# Midnight Musings

By

## MAGDA HERZBERGER

COVER AND INTERIOR ILLUSTRATIONS
by MONICA A. WOLFSON

To my very special
longtime friend
Ildiko,
With love and friendship
Magda
September 9, 2016

Austin Texas

# Midnight Musings

Groundbreaking Press
8305 Arboles Circle
Austin, Texas 78737
512-657-8780
www.groundbreaking.com

ISBN: 978-0-9831030-5-9

First Edition

Senior Editor
Barbara Foley

Book Design & Production
M. Kevin Ford

Music Production
Tim Spivey

Cover and Interior Illustrations
Monica A. Wolfson

Cover Design & Production
M. Kevin Ford

# Dedication

*To my Beloved Family*

*My husband, Eugene E. Herzberger, M.D.*
*Our son, Henry*
*Our daughter, Monica*
*Our grandchildren, Nathan and Mira Ma*
*Our great-granddaughter, Erzi Nicole*

# *Acknowledgements*

My heartfelt gratitude goes to my husband, Eugene E. Herzberger, M.D.

My special thanks to my dear friend, Maggie Smith, C.D.T.

My gratitude and appreciation to my daughter, Monica A. Wolfson, M.E.D.T., for all her efforts in creating and drawing the cover and interior illustrations featured in my book.

My special thanks and gratitude to my dear longtime friend, James P. Moore, Jr., author of the highly acclaimed book, *One Nation Under God: The History of Prayer in America,* Professor at the McDonough School of Business at Georgetown University and a former U.S. Assistant Secretary of Commerce, for all his efforts in writing the compelling and eloquent preface in my book. And also for his other suggestions and constructive criticism.

I am most grateful for the constant support of my publisher, Brad Fregger, and my senior editor, Barbara Foley.

My deepest appreciation to M. Kevin Ford for the interior design and production of my book.

My sincere gratitude to Tim Spivey for the music production for my book.

# Preface

The hour of midnight has always struck us with a sense of solitude, mystery, disquiet, and awe. It divides yesterday from tomorrow. It heralds in the new and punctuates the old. It lends itself to deep introspection on every human level, giving greater definition to who and what we are and from where we have come and where we are going.

The apt title of *Midnight Musings* brings together the prodigious, expansive, and real-life reflections of Magda Herzberger, an extraordinary figure by any measure. She sits alone in the company of her thoughts—past, present, and to come—and reaches out eloquently and movingly to readers from all walks of life. If each one of us is the sum total of everything we have ever experienced in our lives, Magda brings much to the table. We feel privileged to enter into her world, one that unfolds through a variety of poems steeped in reality, fantasy, quest, and profound faith.

While most teenagers are just beginning to explore what adulthood is all about, facing adolescent growing pains, Magda Herzberger was thrust into the world of the Holocaust and the horrors of three concentration camps as she was forced to face the worst traits of humankind and her own mortality. When most young people are launching their professional careers and laying the foundations for their future among family and friends, Magda was living for endless months on a foreign, forbidden beach under primitive conditions, tending to the medical needs of hundreds of refugees awaiting their newly created home in Israel. And then with her physician-husband, Gene, the rock and love of her life, she picked up stakes one more time and arrived on the shores of a different kind of promised land.

And so with her *Midnight Musings*, Magda takes us on a remarkable journey that would be unfamiliar to us otherwise. We are witness to the shadows of despair and the joys of rebirth of a remarkable person's introspections.

Because we know at the outset of *Midnight Musings* of the spiritual depth, resilience, and fulfillment that Magda would ultimately find, we appreciate all the more the highs and lows that her poems express. If she can traverse the land mines that fate has put in her path and find personal peace, she surely has proven to us that we can do the same.

Clearly none of us has or ever will experience the kind of life Magda has led. Nonetheless, for those reading her poetry at an early stage in their lives, they will find glimpses of life's joys, tangled webs, and pitfalls. For those who are older, there will be a knowing familiarity and understanding, at least in part, of her encounters.

The initial selection of poems gives us a brief look into the pathways of Magda's mind and her overarching perspective which is quickly followed by the disturbing intrusions that penetrate her world. "Deformed gnomes," "grotesque figures," and "evil spirits" make unwelcome appearances as they taunt and test her.

But these verses of anguish are followed by those reflecting the profound, deep faith that is at the core of Magda's ability to survive adversity. Thoughts of God's providence give way to petition. Prayers banish desperation.

She makes clear that she can survive anything if she knows that her Creator will only steer her through "life's intricate maze."

From there we are absorbed into the world of Magda's recollections. There is the warm sound of a grand piano, the joyful sight of huge pears falling from a tree in her grandparents' yard, and the rolling tears on her face in the last hour of her dying grandmother. We are transported throughout this section from her childhood to her later years, which gives us an inkling of the legacy she has built over many years.

Some of the most endearing poetry in this collection has to do with nature. Now spending part of the year in the deserts of Arizona and the other part in the mountains of Colorado, Magda has much from which to draw for inspiration. Her encounters with herds of big-horned sheep, the palms of a tall blue spruce, red-tailed hawks, and "winter's crystals sparkling like precious stones" act either as metaphors or represent just the sheer joy of discovering God's continuing gifts to the world.

Her poetry does not lack for pure fun either. "Daydreams" takes us on a ride of Magda's imagination in the realm of fantasy where "nothing is barred from me," and that includes becoming a mountain, a gentle breeze, a typhoon, a beautiful princess, and a wise prophet with a long white beard. Her "Advice to a Housewife" is sheer delight with the counsel, one suspects based on experience, to occasionally "let the dishes pile up, beds undone, relax, and have fun!"

But her wisdom is always present in every one of her

verses like the short but profound "Separate Entities" in which she writes,

> Look for a star,
> Call it your own—
> It will be yours
> Only till dawn—

> Search for an ideal,
> Call it your star—
> It will shine day and night
> Wherever you are—

Her final section, "A Glimpse into Life," brings to closure the poems that come before it; giving pause to what Magda has come to learn over a lifetime which will soon enter its tenth decade. "Mystery," "Uncertainty," and "Unanswered Questions" provide just a sample of her unfinished business. While there is always a tinge of regret that life cannot proceed forever in unlocking new doors and adventures, she nonetheless conveys a genuine sense of profound contentment. Her deep spiritual devotion places her future squarely in God's hands where it has always been. For us, her readers, there too is a bittersweet sense that we cannot travel with her more—at least for now. In reading her book, cover to cover, we cannot help but feel blessed that she has opened new doors for us while taking us by the hand.

There is one final surprise, however, that Magda provides for us, an Afterword she calls "A Look into the Life of the Sea." After living for more than a year in primitive tents with other refugees on the shores of Cyprus in 1948, awaiting permission to immigrate to the newly created state of Israel, she developed a romance for the sea.

That experience is reflected in her writing verse and composing music to bring together the memories and emotions that the Aegean Sea brought out for her. For someone untrained in musical composition, particularly with full symphony, soloists, and choir, this is quite an achievement. The calm and undulating rhythms of the waves at one moment, and their relentless crashes against the rocks at another, can be felt throughout her piece and within the verses of her poetry. It is a delight to read the lyrics and to imagine the sounds of the music that emerge from the impressions she gained almost 55 years ago when life was rugged, her future uncertain, and the presence of the sea so pervasive.

Perhaps there is no better way to summarize Magda's poetic journey for her readers than to quote the last lines of "Fantasies" where she writes,

> I renounced all earthly pleasures
> Ambitions and glory—
> I found peace and harmony
> And answered the question,
> To be or not to be.
>
> And now it is for you to decide
> On the other side,
> If I was right or wrong,
> Weak or strong—

Or, just a dreamer
On a beautiful day
In summer.

I think it is fair to say that her readers will decide for themselves. *Midnight Musings* is Magda's gift to us all.

The Honorable James P. Moore, Jr.
Washington, D. C.
February 2013

The Biography of The Honorable James P. Moore, Jr.

James P. Moore, Jr., has enjoyed a varied career in government, business, and academia. He was nominated by President Ronald Reagan and confirmed by the U.S. Senate to several senior government positions, including U.S. Assistant Secretary of Commerce. During his tenure in government, he negotiated a number of international agreements on behalf of the United States, including the last trade economic agreement with the Soviet Union.

Today, Mr. Moore sits as a professor at the McDonough School of Business at Georgetown University, where he teaches international business as well as ethics and management and leadership. He also sits on several corporate and nonprofit boards and is a featured guest commentator on CNBC and other cable and television networks.

In addition he is the award-winning author of *One Nation Under God: The History of Prayer in America*, which was made into the miniseries Prayer in America for public television. His most recent book, *The Treasury of American Prayer*, also won critical acclaim for capturing the essence of the country's spirituality through the prayers of its people. In addition to invocations in the collection from such individuals as Benjamin Franklin, Emily Dickinson, Harry Truman, and Conrad Hilton, there are those of Magda Herzberger.

# Table of Contents

**PART 3**

# Author's Note

Poetry is the music of the spoken word. Poems are the songs of life. The birth of a poem is a miraculous, mysterious, spontaneous, and natural subconscious manifestation. I can compare it best to the miracle of life. It is a sudden, unexpected revelation.

I began writing poetry in 1963 and continued throughout these many years to do so. It became one of my great fulfillments in life.

As a poet, I feel that I am like a photographer. The camera lens is my mind through which the images appear, and then I develop them into the spoken words, which rise from the Immortal Spirit.

Sometimes I focus my camera and take pictures from the outside world surrounding us, directing my lens into the different corners of life.

Other times I take photos depicting the many aspects of the inner world of my soul. Behind each of my poems in my book, *Midnight Musings*, there is a story to be told and experienced.

One of my main goals in life is to instill love for poetry in the hearts of the people.

*Magda Herzberger*
*February 2013*

# Prologue

Life and death are the opposite forces directing man's destiny. Each day somewhere the birth of a new life is celebrated, and each day somewhere the mourners close the eyes of those who depart from this world forever.

Life is the greatest miracle created by God and the most precious gift entrusted to humanity to be cherished and respected, but it is unpredictable, constantly changing with the tides of time. As long as there is the spark of life within us, we change. The tides are pulling us sometimes into the stormy sea and other times they push us out into the warm, soft sand. Life is like the ocean with its high and low tides, its serene and stormy periods. Death is the inevitable fate of man. We must accept that our destiny is carved at birth, and that we are merely visitors on earth. I learned a great deal about life and death in the German concentration camps where I was a prisoner during World War II.

# Prologue

*Life is but a brief encounter*
*With the joys of earthly fun ...*
*On the wheel of fate*
*Our destiny is spun ...*
*Delicate threads of ecstasy*
*Mixed with coarse fibers of doom and agony*
*Are woven on the loom of existence*
*By the invisible hands of Almighty God ...*
*The finished cloth*
*Stamped with our blood*
*Never becomes our property ...*
*We are allowed only*
*To take a short glimpse*
*Of its beauty ...*
*Before death takes it away*
*At the end of our last day ...*

# Part 1

Magda Herzberger

# Creativity

Creativity takes place in the deep, silent chambers of the mind where the waves of thoughts roll. ...

## Creativity

The writer enters imagination's den
And picks up papers and pen.
Seated by fantasy's spacious desk,
The bodies of thoughts dance
And bare themselves in his mind,
Like strippers in a burlesque.
More and more words appear
On the blank white sheets,
And the Muse greets the poet
With open arms,
Healing balms,
And creative alms.

Magda Herzberger

# Endless Night

The daylight is out of sight,
It is the middle of the night,
But a pair of eyes
Red like fire
Never tire—
They keep on fighting, staring,
And no rest ever sharing—

On sleepless nights
Anguish starts,
And blue circles in the air
Keep on turning—
You count the minutes, the seconds,
The hours which follow,
And you wish of no tomorrow.
Even the daybreak seems like the night,
Dark and bleak
And never bright.

# Reflections

Hit by the gusty winds of fate
And chilled by the cold hand of destiny,
My heart shrivels like a flower in fall.
On the threshold of life's autumn I stand,
And now I can understand
That each day falls a golden leaf,
Life is precious but brief.
Time is ageless without limit,
Stretching into the infinite.

Now I can see the innocence of childhood,
The beauty and liveliness
Of youth and adolescence,
And the colorful years of maturity.

Oh, my soul, you are still a dreamer,
A flame and its ashes,
Tame and wild,
Trusting forever like a child.

Magda Herzberger

# Illusion

In the dark room
No one stirred,
Only the sound
Of my fast breathing
I heard—
Fantasy was playing tricks on me—
I thought you were here
Listening to my pounding heart
And feeling the warmth
Of my body—
But, I was alone
With the shadow
Of a distant memory—

# Visions

There are times when our somber thoughts carry us to the desolate, arid, and forsaken deserts of loneliness, where we are trapped and haunted by the dark, foreboding shadows of melancholy, as my following poems express.

## Desolate

*The specters of the night appear,*
*The sky is clear.*
*Where are the joys of yesterday?*
*Stretched out on my bed today,*
*I listen to the ticking of the clock and pray*
*That sleep will come my way,*
*But I can clearly see*
*That another sleepless night*
*Is in store for me.*

*My thoughts travel far away,*
*Searching for the happiness of yesterday.*
*The past unfolds its wings and gradually*
*A feeling of sadness and loss descend upon me.*

*I find myself in a strange. unfamiliar land*
*Called the country of melancholy,*

Magda Herzberger

*Where all the colors are blue*
*And dark is the heaven's hue,*
*Where somber rains of tears*
*Constantly fall,*
*It is the place of the tortured soul.*

*There is no peace in this territory,*
*The battles of painful emotions*
*Go on and on.*
*Here there is no bright sun,*
*But darkness reigns*
*And destruction rules.*
*It is the land of the lonely,*
*The land of the fools.*

*It is the place*
*Where the evil spirits dwell,*
*Leading you to the ports of hell.*

# Destitute

My thoughts are lost in space—
There is no trace of earth
Or any sign of years.
No human sound reaches my ears.
The hard ground of the old planet
Where I was born,
With all its mist, dust and gold
Is torn out of my memory
And dumped into the realm of infinity.

I can't see anymore
Life's distant sandy shore,
Nor the wrinkled face of time.
Neither can I hear the clink
Of existence's chime.

I am delivered to loneliness
And thrown into the arms
Of solitude and isolation,
Witnessing the cessation
Of joy and happiness.

My spirit is trapped
By the celestial firmament.

# Magda Herzberger

*Only the vapors*
*Of the thin atmosphere*
*Surround my mind,*
*And I wander*
*Amidst the countless drops of water,*
*Passing the dark clouds of melancholy,*
*Crossing the borders of sanity,*
*Where pushed by the strong winds of madness*
*And struck by the lightning of black emotions,*
*I fall into nothingness.*

# Haunting

*Invisible phantoms of fear*
*Twist my mind*
*And grind my heart.*
*Deformed gnomes suddenly appear,*
*Whispering all kinds of lies into my ear,*
*Clouding my vision*
*With the fog of illusion.*

*I hear them say:*
*"Pray for your sanity!*
*We are the grotesque figures*
*Of madness,*
*The bodies of horror,*
*The specters of terror.*
*We can tear the human soul apart,*
*By starting the fire of despair in the heart.*
*We have wings to hover in the air*
*And obscure your sight.*
*Our wings don't melt in the sun,*
*Thus we can rob the day of light.*

*"We came to disturb your sleep,*
*To make you suffer and weep.*
*Madness upon you stares...*
*We are the ghosts of nightmares!*

# Magda Herzberger

No one is strong enough
To stop our intrusion
Into your room.
We are powerful and tough.
We are the spirits of doom
And the specters of delusion.

"We are the children of your thoughts,
A part of your flesh and blood.
We are visitors sent to you by God
To remind you of the dark pit of emotions,
To make you feel the power of delusions,
To let you know
That within the painful stream of life,
And the magic world of dream,
Dark shadows of the underground
Roam around and scream."

Oh, gnomes of my weary heart,
Don't tear me apart!
Return to your dark caves,
Don't open fantasy's mad door.
Let me find peace,
Don't torment me anymore.
Your laughter is cutting my breath,
I feel a sharp pain in my chest.

*You invoke in me*
*The fear of death.*
*Please go away and let me rest.*

*"We are free to come and go,*
*And to follow you*
*Whenever we desire.*
*Once you evoke us, you have no control*
*Over your soul.*
*We will tear you apart.*
*We ignore your cries,*
*Within our strong grip*
*Sanity dies.*
*Madness is born*
*And peace, beauty, calm,*
*Happiness, stability,*
*Ambition and reality,*
*Into the depths of hell's flames are thrown."*

*Spirits of agonizing nightmares,*
*Please depart and leave me alone!*

Magda Herzberger

# Possessed

Darkness swallows the bright light,
Somber shadows dim my sight,
The deformed gnomes of destiny
Surround me,
Chanting the songs
Of blasphemy.
Glowing red eyes stare at me—
The evil creatures of the underground
Follow me around,
On my peace of mind they pound.

"Messengers of calamity and hate,
You have no right to guide my fate!
Don't open hell's flaming gate,
Where the devil in his black attire
Burns the souls on the hot pyre.
Destruction is his desire."

"Hell's ports are always wide open
Where the entering spirits are broken.
The token of truth is crushed
And the victims are rushed
To the king of darkness,
And then tossed into an abyss
Filled with weird sounds,
Where the devil's laughter resounds."

# Intrusion

Threatening, ominous thoughts
Emerging from the somber, dark and deep
Chambers of my soul
Upon me descend,
Robbing my sleep.
I am at my wit's end.
My heartbeat is racing,
My body is shaking.

I hear the bells
Enclosed in my spirit's black towers,
Tolling existence's passing hours.
My ears are bound
To the deafening sound
Of life's wild rhythm.
Peace and calm I can't find.
I am losing my mind
And my freedom,
Leaving my sanity behind.

I am confused, dazed and perplexed,
And start to pray
Asking for a way
To control my mounting fear and anxiety,
Waiting for the maddening sound
To lose its intensity.

# Magda Herzberger

But until then,
I have to bear
My suffering and pain,
And endure the stress and strain.
I cry out loud,
I walk around
And pound my room's wall,
Waiting for the call
Of peace and harmony
To stop my agony.

# Imprisoned

*On silent nights*
*When the distant stars*
*Open their sparkling eyes,*
*And the yellow moon*
*Reveals its melancholic face,*
*The lonely heart cries*
*Locked in its cage,*
*Crippled by age,*
*A helpless prisoner of time—*

*But, once it was free and in its prime,*
*Beating with vigor*
*The fast rhythm of life—*
*And now, it is doomed and forsaken,*
*Its livelihood taken,*
*Robbed of love and pride,*
*Pushed aside,*
*Condemned to solitude.*

*Weary heart, where is your fortitude?*
*The hand of fate*
*Slammed on you*
*Its iron gate,*
*Extinguished your fire,*
*And left you to expire*
*In the prison of the years—*

17

# Magda Herzberger

*I hear your cry*
*And streaks of salty tears*
*Run down my cheeks—*
*I turn to the lighted sky*
*Asking for mercy—*
*There is no reply.*
*But I can see from afar*
*The flashing light*
*Of a falling star—*

*I mourn you,*
*Battered heart,*
*Slave of destiny,*
*Bound forever*
*To captivity.*

# Someone Listens

My eyes follow
The grey contours
And the slow movements
Of the wooden limbs and twigs
Stripped of their green garments—
They are lonely, naked, cold,
Silent and reserved—

My mind is blurred
By melancholy's opaque fog—
My heart is stiff and old
Like a discarded useless log—
My dreams were shattered,
Trust and love were battered,
Self-esteem undermined—
Peace of mind I can't find.

Life is like a floating phantom
Drifting here and there at random—
My spirit is searching for a clearing,
But behind the vapory mist
Only madness is lurking—

I desperately shout:
"Is there a way out?

## Magda Herzberger

*Is there a cure*
*For a tortured soul?*
*Who will listen*
*To the suffering spirit's last call?*
*Is there a clue*
*For the rescue*
*Of a lost wanderer*
*Who seeks relief*
*From pending grief?*
*Who is helpless like a falling leaf—*
*Are all efforts in vain?*
*Is someone listening to the lament*
*Of a mortal in pain*
*Directed to the witnessing firmament?*

*"Only the Creator above*
*Who possesses the flames*
*Of compassion and love*
*Hears the cry,*
*And opens the golden ports*
*Of the sky*
*To receive His creation*
*At the world's highest*
*And most luminous station."*

# Death of the Poet

*When the poet dies,*
*No one sees*
*The mourning trees*
*Wiping their tears.*
*No one hears the flowers cry,*
*Whispering a sad goodbye*
*To their departed friend,*
*Whom the earth will hold forever*
*In its hand.*

*The funeral is held*
*In nature's cathedral,*
*Where the birds perched*
*On high branches*
*Sing the requiem:*
*"Triste Diem, Triste Diem."*

*And below, the chorus of frogs*
*Seated on old logs*
*Softly repeat,*
*"Croak, croak, croak,*
*We are heartbroke."*
*The orchestra of crickets*
*Accompanies the wailing sounds*
*Of sadness and despair,*
*Resounding in the air.*

21

# Magda Herzberger

*The tall evergreens and cedars*
*Solemnly stand by*
*Under the cloudless sky,*
*Grieving the loss*
*Of their cherished friend,*
*Who fell into death's hand.*
*Looking with sadness*
*At the burial ground,*
*Where the poet will remain*
*Forever earthbound,*
*Where darkness and silence*
*Will prevail.*

*No sounds will ever reach*
*The deep underground,*
*Where only death will hail*
*It's victory*
*Over the poet's dead body.*

*But the poet's spirit*
*Will never die,*
*It will leave the earth*
*And rise up to the sky.*

# The Power of Prayer

As we are treading the torturous roads of existence, we ask for God's assistance. How else could we face all the difficulties and unpleasant surprises which destiny keeps in store for us!

Our faith in the power of our Creator gives us strength to carry the heavy loads of challenges which we meet in our lifetime.

If we are true believers and we open freely our hearts to the Lord, then our prayers will be heard and our wishes will come true. Our dreams and goals we set for ourselves will materialize.

Each of us has a different request from the Almighty. My following prayers convey my personal pleas to the King of the Universe.

## Plea for Help

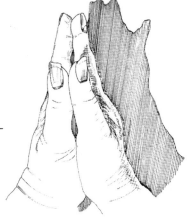

*My mind is on fire,*
*My spirit is in flames,*
*Destiny is playing on me*
*Its wild tricks and games—*
*The volcano of anger*
*Erupts in my heart,*
*Its hot flowing lava*
*Tears me apart—*

# Magda Herzberger

*I fight for my life in vain—*
*The melting rocks of destruction*
*Are burning my brain*
*And blinding my reason—*
*Trapped in their prison,*
*Tortured by relentless agony and pain,*
*Robbed of peace and happiness,*
*I am driven to madness—*

*O God, upon you I call,*
*Please, comfort my suffering soul,*
*And appease my pain.*
*Relieve me from this agonizing*
*Stress and strain—*
*Help me to survive,*
*Please keep me alive!*

*Only you can heal*
*My injured spirit.*
*To you, my Creator, I appeal—*
*Perform on me a great miracle.*
*Push away from me any obstacle—*
*Extend your helping hand*
*And let peace and harmony*
*Upon me descend—*

24

# Midnight Musings

*Keep away the fury*
*Of deep, painful emotions*
*And help me find for myself*
*The right solutions—*
*Extinguish the raging fire*
*And instill in me the desire*
*To create the most beautiful*
*Songs and verse—*

*King of the Universe,*
*Let the flames subside*
*And be my Protector and Guide—*
*Let the ocean of creativity*
*Inundate my body and soul.*
*Almighty, help me to attain my goal—*
*Help me to forgive those*
*Who wronged me unjustly—*

*Let love replace all trace*
*Of resentment and grief.*
*Let my anger and hatred be brief—*
*Let the rays of hope*
*Shine upon my bleeding heart*
*And let tranquility conquer my soul.*
*King of the Universe,*
*Please, listen to my call—*
*And don't let me fall*
*Into the pit of depression.*

## Magda Herzberger

*Make me anew,*
*Make my wishes come true—*
*Let me experience the joy*
*Of spiritual resurrection.*
*Lead me to the path*
*Of gentility and affection—*
*Free me from my haunting obsession*
*Hold me under Your protection.*

# Meditations

O Lord, be merciful
And kind to me.
Let me maintain
My physical strengths,
My good health, and sanity.
Help me to retain
Even in my old age
The spark of creativity
And my mental ability
To compose music and verse,
Singing and reciting
The beauty of the universe.

Don't let me change
My innate personality,
Save me from lapses of memory,
And from mental deterioration.
Grant me these attributes
As long as I am destined
To reside on life's station.

Please watch over the safety
Of my beloved husband,
My loyal loving partner,
With whom I joined hands
A long time ago.

27

# Magda Herzberger

*Let us be always together*
*And never apart,*
*Because we have by now*
*A common heart.*

*We are linked to each other*
*By the many years*
*Through which we shared*
*Our joys and tears,*
*Our tribulations, victories,*
*Successes and fears.*

*My Creator, please*
*Listen to my prayer*
*And send us from above,*
*The precious gifts of happiness,*
*Good health, and love.*

# Personal Prayer

My Creator,
Ruler of the Universe,
To You Almighty, I address my verse.
Send me your Guiding Light
To illuminate my dark soul,
And please help me to find my goal.

Let the flood of love
Overflow my being.
Teach me the art of kindness
And forgiveness.
Divert evil's poison arrows from my heart,
Let them pass me by.
Let me envision Your Sacred Hands
Encompassing the earth, the sea and the sky.

Fulfill my wish
And reveal Your Face
In the heart of a rose.
Almighty, please teach me to compose
True music and write beautiful poetry
And genuine prose,
So that I can sing to humanity
Of Your glory, strengths, pity and mercy.
I will convey the power of Your Blessings
Hour after hour.

# Magda Herzberger

*My only God*
*Who created my flesh and blood,*
*Please hear my prayer*
*And register me*
*In the book of life and creativity.*

# Psalm III

*God, my Creator,*
*Performer of great miracles,*
*Grant me the foresight*
*Of ancient oracles.*

*Almighty Ruler of Heaven's Kingdom,*
*Bestow upon me the gift of wisdom,*
*And help me to find my way*
*Year after year,*
*Through life's intricate maze.*
*Please clear the haze*
*Of doubt and fear.*
*Instill the rays of hope in my heart,*
*Don't let my spirit fall apart.*

*Let me walk with confidence*
*The tortuous streets of the future,*
*Be my Guardian and Counseling Teacher.*
*Don't let me stray*
*From the right direction.*
*Plant in my soul the precious seeds*
*Of faith and affection.*
*Keep me away from evil thoughts and deeds.*
*Destroy the harmful weeds*
*Of cruelty, conceit and greed.*

# Magda Herzberger

*Let me shine like the full moon,*
*Let my spirit bloom*
*Like a flower in May.*
*Save me from confusion and disarray.*

*Dissolve the clouds of distress,*
*Let contentment and happiness*
*Descend upon me,*
*So that I can see clearly*
*The path I was destined to follow.*

*Reflect upon me the bright glow*
*Of inspiration*
*And help me find*
*My true vocation.*

*Let me create the most beautiful*
*Music and verse*
*Glorifying Your Sacred Name,*
*And the mysteries of the universe.*
*O Lord my Protector,*
*To You I pray,*
*Please send the Muse my way.*

# Psalm IV

Eternal Spirit,
Governing my body,
Set me free of pettiness,
Let me follow the path of love,
Faith and forgiveness.
Let my soul be tender, but sturdy.
Please give me strength, Almighty,
To carry the heavy loads
Of aches and sorrow,
And the burdens of tomorrow.
Let my joy of life be thorough.
Envelope my being
In the golden shield of joy,
That no man on earth can destroy.

Let my heart yield
To the beauty of Your Creation,
Let loose the bounds
Of my imagination.
Let me soar the heights of Heaven
And enter once more the Garden of Eden,
Where the roses of knowledge
And happiness bloom.

# Magda Herzberger

*Ruler of the Universe,*
*Please grant my wish*
*And destroy my gloom.*

*I am worn and beaten*
*Asking Your help.*
*God save me from fear,*
*Man's worst enemy,*
*Killer of the mind and body,*
*And guide me*
*To the road of eternity.*

*Oh, Lord, set me free*
*From the prison of depression,*
*And perform on me*
*A spiritual resurrection.*

# Memory Lane

Old memories live behind the doors of time. Only our thoughts can reach them by traveling freely through the realm of the years. There is no barrier for the spirit. It can be present anywhere at any time.

## Reminiscences

*The whispers of thoughts*
*Echo in the forest of my mind.*
*Nostalgia and melancholy*
*Cast their shadows upon me.*
*Episodes of my life appear*
*Upon the screen of my memory.*
*They are projected over and over*
*Like scenes from an old worn movie.*
*A network of dreams*
*Float on the stream*
*Of recollection.*

*I can see your image clearly,*
*Standing proudly*
*As a young man beside me,*
*Taking the vow of holy matrimony,*

# Magda Herzberger

*Placing the marriage ring on my finger*
*And uttering the sacred commitment*
*Of accepting me as your lawful wife,*
*For better or worse,*
*In sickness and health.*
*I hear the music of love*
*And the sound of the wedding bells*
*Filling the place.*
*I look at your happy face.*

*I feel my throbbing heart*
*Repeating the sacred oath,*
*Accepting you as my beloved husband,*
*Asking God to bless us both*
*With love and devotion,*
*Joining our hands*
*To walk together side by side*
*Through the wilderness of life,*
*United by the seal of affection,*
*Promising to cherish*
*Passion's precious token,*
*Never to let our loyalty*
*Ever be broken,*
*And to keep the door of love*
*Forever open.*

*Sixty-five years have passed*
*Since our wedding day,*
*So let us pray*
*For many more,*
*And let us keep forever*
*The promise we made*
*To each other*
*A long time before.*

Magda Herzberger

# Exploring the Heights

*So many times I climbed the high mountains*
*Through the years—*
*On their silent slopes*
*I lost my worries and fears*
*And I found happiness and peace—*
*I crossed their rocky surface*
*In summer's heat,*
*On my two feet.*
*And in winter on skis—*
*I was sliding in their deep virgin snow,*
*Entrapped in the sun's bright glow—*

*I stood on their magnificent peaks*
*Facing the sky—*
*I passed by*
*The dense forests of evergreens*
*And the green meadows*
*Scattered with blooming wildflowers—*
*I witnessed the sunrise*
*In the early morning hours,*
*And the sunset's fiery multicolored reflections*
*Bewitched my eyes—*
*I heard the high-pitched cries*
*Of the mountain jays*
*And the melodies of the songbirds—*

38

*I saw the herds*
*Of the big-horned sheep,*
*The crowd of the white mountain goats,*
*And the elk families*
*Grazing on the steep shoulders*
*And climbing the rough boulders—*

*I watched the deer leap*
*And run up and down*
*With such ease and grace,*
*Stopping now and then*
*To look at my face—*

*I drank the pure water*
*Of the fresh mountain streams—*
*A wonderland unfolded before me,*
*The kind you experience in your dreams.*
*I marveled in God's great creation,*
*Looking at a world which extends*
*Beyond imagination—*

Magda Herzberger

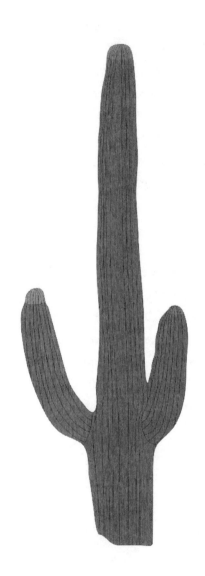

# Desert Land

*Dark, ominous clouds hover*
*Over the distant mountains—*
*A gray mist envelopes the sky,*
*The sun retreats saying goodbye—*
*Strong winds are howling,*
*The birds are flying*
*With great agitation*
*And swift acceleration,*
*Having the sensation*
*That a violent storm is on its way—*
*For their safety they pray—*

*The sound of thunder is heard,*
*The menace and concern*
*Of every bird—*
*Lightning illuminates the earth,*
*Giving birth to heaven's drummer—*
*Heavy rain pours down,*
*Running through the gutter,*
*Pounding its large drops*
*On the rooftops,*
*Hitting the ground*
*And everything around—*

## Magda Herzberger

The tall, huge, straight, ancient saguaros,
Looking like giant Hebrew menorahs,
Are storing the water
Inside their pleated folds,
Holding out their curled, thick arms
And prickly palms—

Looking through the window
Of my room,
I see the yellow flowers
Of the brittle bush in bloom,
The fuchsia bougainvillea,
The purple lantana,
The white fragrant blossoms
Of the acacia,
The delicate blue rosemaries,
And the luscious leaves
Of the Australian bottle trees—

My thoughts wander,
Evoking scenes from the past—
I try to trace the memories
Of my former dwelling place—
I see in my imagination
The impressive, voluminous maple trees,
The squirrels running up and down
Their wrinkled trunks,

*The big mass of green grass,*
*The blooming petunias, dahlias,*
*The bright marigolds,*
*And all the beauty nature holds—*

*But now in my new residence in desert land*
*I enjoy the peace and silence at hand—*
*Springtime is here*
*And the desert is awakening—*
*The quails are screaming,*
*The birds are singing,*
*The great horned owls are sleeping,*
*Waiting to hunt at night*
*And to eat everything in sight—*
*They like to stay perched and hoot*
*On the top of our chimney lined with soot*
*Before they swoop down to the ravine*
*For their food and loot—*

*The red-tailed hawks*
*Are also looking for their prey,*
*From our roof they fly away—*
*What a great privilege*
*To have such visitors,*
*Such magnificent predators—*
*They are brave, dignified and free,*
*Soaring the heights*
*In their flights—*

# Magda Herzberger

I learned to enjoy the desert,
Its bushes and trees—
The colorful creosote,
The blooming cholla,
The red salvia,
The mesquite and palo verde trees,
The ironwood, the cactus flowers,
The Arizona poppies,
The exotic orange blossoms of the ocotillo,
The vibrant penstemon,
The desert marigolds,
And all the vegetation
The desert land holds—

I like the shining sun,
The cool breeze,
And living in a climate
Where I never freeze—
I like the mountain ridges,
The washes, the palm trees,
The buzzing of the bees,
The roaming coyotes,
The humming birds,
The javelina herds—

# Midnight Musings

The *diamondback rattlesnakes and scorpions*
*Are not my favorites,*
*But my heart beats*
*The rhythm of love*
*For all the living creatures*
*Below and above—*
*For all the trees, bushes and flowers,*
*For the spring and summer showers,*
*For the blue sky,*
*For the clouds which pass by—*

*It is so wonderful to be alive*
*And to see all the beauty around me,*
*To listen to nature's symphony*
*And to touch the precious treasures*
*Of God's creation,*
*On my temporary earthly station—*

Magda Herzberger

# Remembrances

Trembling leaves
Chilled by icy winds
Are swaying to and fro
In front of my window—
My eyes follow
The naked frosty limbs.
My thoughts are sinking
Into the hollow of the past—
The familiar ticking
Of the old clock is fading,
As my senses unlock
The doors of time—
My spirit wanders
On the field of reminiscences.
Images are flashing
On the screen of my mind—

I find the forgotten,
Abandoned house
Where once I dwelt.
I open its sealed doors
With the key of memory—
I see cobwebs hanging low
And mildew growing on its walls.

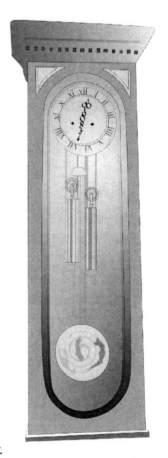

As darkness falls,
I detect shadows moving in—
A flame within my body and soul is burning —
Suddenly this old building
Becomes once more
The way it used to be before—
Filled with light and love,

With life and beauty—
Surrounded by a happy family.
I hear the voices of my parents—
I feel the presence
Of peace and harmony.
I hear clearly
The music of my youth—
Its soothing melody
Resonates through my heart.
I listen to the gentle voices
Of childhood and adolescence—
Singing to me
The song of reverie:

"You are only dreaming,
Illusions are deceiving—
If you dwell in them too long,
They may rob your sanity—
Return to reality!

# Magda Herzberger

*But, come back*
*Once in a while to me,*
*Your true and loyal friend,*
*Your childhood memory.*
*You will always find me here*
*Year after year—*
*My spirit lives in this old home*
*Erecting its golden dome—"*

# Abandonment

In the early morning's chill,
She ran down the green hill,
Holding in her hand
A trembling daffodil—
A big smile crossed her pretty face,
Her blue eyes reflected youth,
Innocence and grace—
A gentle breeze teased
Her dark long hair,
While blooming flowers fragranced
The fresh air—
The sun displayed
Its golden ring—
The birds sang their songs
Of joyful spring—

She greeted the blue sky
With a happy outcry.
A feeling of great love in her heart stirred
And the haunting melody of life she heard—
She opened her arms
To embrace the world—
And held out her hand
Waiting for a butterfly to land—

49

Magda Herzberger

# Recollections

Childhood memories are like genuine precious pearls, maintaining their value and beauty through the passing years. I still remember clearly the house of my grandparents, the orchard where I used to play with my cousins, the white room with the grand piano, the happy and carefree times I experienced as a young child.

Many years have passed by since then, but I can still evoke the places, the people, and the feelings of joy and happiness in those early years of my life. They were imprinted forever into my memory.

## Childhood Memory

*In the white room*
*With the grand piano*
*I listened to a solo.*
*I watched the fingers*
*Move rapidly*
*From right to left,*
*From left to right,*
*Striking the white*
*And black keys*
*Firmly.*
*It was my aunt playing—*

# Magda Herzberger

*The room was filled with music,*
*And images started moving*
*In front of me:*
*A river, with its gentle ripples,*
*A quiet summer afternoon,*
*With birds chirping,*
*And crickets singing.*
*Here and there*
*A butterfly,*
*Blooming flowers*
*Stretching their stems*
*And turning their heads*
*Toward the sky—*

*I saw a cat*
*through the window,*
*Passing the hollow*
*Old oak*
*With its shabby cloak.*
*The dog barked*
*And chased his enemy away—*

*I wish I could stay*
*Once more in the house*
*Of my grandparents,*
*And meet again*
*All the friendly tenants*
*Of the yard:*

The orchard,
The flowers,
The grass,
The tall linden trees,
To hear again
The buzzing
Of the bees,
To relive
The happy memories,
And the curiosity
Of the child—

Farewell
To all of these,
But they still live
In the hidden corners
Of the past
Where they will
Forever last.

Magda Herzberger

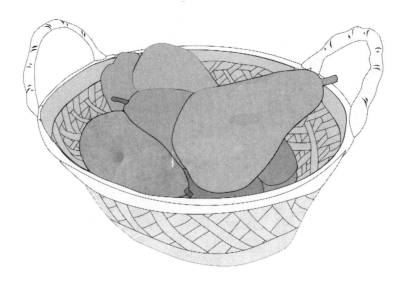

# Harvest Time

Certain childhood memories are imprinted deeply into our minds and they live on and on, having the ability to project themselves any time at random on the screen of our imagination.

I can still see after all these years the old pear tree in my grandparents' yard. It was an old friend delivering its fruits faithfully each year. I can still feel the joy and happiness I experienced in my childhood when I collected in the month of September the big Bartlett pears in my little basket. I was rejoicing the harvest together with my cousins.

## The Old Pear Tree

*I still remember the old pear tree*
*Standing majestically*
*In my grandparents' yard*
*When I, as a small child,*
*Playing with my cousins in the room,*
*Suddenly flew out of the house fast*
*Like a witch on a broom.*
*We shook the old tree violently,*
*Waiting for its fruits to fall, impatiently.*
*We picked up the big pears quickly,*
*Examining each one separately,*

# Magda Herzberger

*Admiring their giant size,*
*Uttering shrieks of surprise.*

*The good old tree*
*Delivered us yearly*
*Its produce faithfully.*
*We looked up at it with pride,*
*Saying loudly,*
*"Here is the best friend*
*Of Grandmother's yard."*
*After all these years,*
*Our laughter mixed with tears,*
*Still echoes in my ears.*

# Flashback

How can I ever forget my dear grandmother? We were such good friends. She always took time to listen to me and give the best advice and guidance she could think of. Now that I have grandchildren of my own, I understand fully the deep affection she felt for me.

I admired her keen intellect, her exceptional physical strength, her ambitious, yet kind, nature, and her great love and devotion to her family.

She was a hardworking woman, tireless, charged continuously with high energy.

Unfortunately, at age 71, she was struck by a debilitating heart ailment. She died a year later at age 72. At that time I was in my mid teens. She spent the last year of her life at our home, confined most of the time to a chair. It was painful for me to see her suffer so much. She had frequent serious heart attacks, sometimes accompanied by a high fever. She often told me that the reason she kept on fighting for her survival was to be a little longer with me and her family.

A week before her death she knew the end was near. The following dialogue tool place between us at her bedside on the day she passed away.

Magda Herzberger

# The Last Hour

"Come, my child,
Can you see that black shadow
By the window?"

"No, there isn't anything there,
Dear Grandmother."

"I can see distinctly a dark figure
Waiting for me—
There he sits on the window frame,
He knows that he will win his game."

"Grandmother, dear Grandmother,
It is only your fever."

"No, there is no mistake,
I can see death's outline
Even when I am wide awake—
He waited for me a whole year,
Sometimes he was so near
That I could hear him whisper in my ear,
'Soon you will be mine'—

"Come here, my dear Granddaughter,
Sit upon my bed,
Put your palm upon my burning head.

*I know this is my last day,*
*So listen to what I have to say—*

*"I was once young, pretty and strong,*
*And filled with so much energy.*
*I thought the whole world was just for me.*
*I married early,*
*And dedicated my life to my family.*
*I loved my husband dearly.*
*We were happy,*
*I raised your father*
*And your uncle decently.*

*"Now I will join your grandfather, finally—*
*And even after death,*
*Love will keep us company—*
*Give me your hand, my loved one,*
*Let us say to each other, goodbye.*
*Keep me always in your memory*
*As the years go by."*

*"Grandmother, Grandmother,*
*Please don't die!*
*I love you so—"*

*"My dear child, don't cry,*
*Some day we all must go."*

Magda Herzberger

# Consumed

Fairy tales and childhood dreams
Float on memory streams
Drifting through the drops of tears—
Then, tossed around
By the current of years,
They land on the silent island
Of reverie—
From there, they lure my sailing heart
Like enticing sirens
To the edge of melancholy—

There, I am bound
To the pyre of yearning
And desire—
While my spirit and body
Are burning,
I hear the last agonizing notes
Of life's sweet melody—
A small pile of ashes
Mark my remains
On the shore of destiny—

# Retrospection

After the long and cold winter months all of us look forward to the arrival of spring. We greet with joy the warm sunshine, the fresh green grass, and the first blooming tulips and daffodils. But not everyone is so fortunate to reach and to enjoy the beauty and wonders of this special time of the year. There are those among us who are stricken by the hand of fate and are forced to exit from life before this beautiful season appears.

The same goes on in the life of nature around us.

I remember what happened to my favorite old willow tree which was bordering our neighbor's property and facing our bedroom window. For many years I admired its impressive crown loaded with drooping, dreamy, luscious leaves and its strong, thick, powerful trunk. It was like an old friend, standing there and waving to me. Then one day sometime in April when I was heading to inspect the first buds of my favorite tree, I discovered to my horror that only a dead stump, a lifeless specter, was facing me. The old willow was gone. I was heartbroken and angry that our neighbors cut it down. Many years have passed by since then, but I can never forget my dear old friend.

Magda Herzberger

# Nostalgia

As Spring sings its joyful melodies,
Fresh buds burst on the waking trees.
Fragrant blossoms unfold
Their furled petals,
And colorful butterflies circle
The blue sky,
While a gentle breeze is passing by—
But where is the old willow?
We used to greet each other
Through my bedroom window—
As the years rolled by
We became such good friends.
Now, its graceful green hands
Will wave to me no more,
No woodpeckers will ever dwell
In its core.
Its crown will no longer shelter
Any robin's nest,
No winter snow will rest
On its breast.
Only a dead stump is facing me—
A lifeless specter, still hanging around,
Clinging to the hard ground.
And yet, my dear old tree,
We can't ever be apart—
You live in my memory,
Bound forever to my heart.

# Strange Encounter in July

A big city like Chicago with its huge skyscrapers and many cultural centers is an interesting place to visit. This large metropolitan area offers a great variety of entertainment to its public. In the daytime, the streets are crowded with people and the heavy, slow-moving traffic pollutes the air. At night, the colorful neon lights are flashing everywhere. The high, illuminated towers become impressive and spectacular. The smoke-stained surfaces of buildings are hidden from the view.

But in my opinion, all the glamour and excitement of a large city are no compensations for the hard and hectic lifestyle to which its inhabitants are constantly exposed. I personally prefer to live in a smaller city where the sun is not obstructed by massive edifices.

We visited Chicago several times through the years. On one of our visits in the month of July, I experienced a strange encounter.

We were staying for a day in a room on the 19th floor of the hotel. It was late afternoon, when peeking through the window, I saw a gray pigeon perched on the sill, facing me. Our eyes met and suddenly I was reminded of the freedom and beauty of a simple world, which was far more appealing and desirable to me than those surrounding stony giants.

Magda Herzberger

# Confrontation

*On the smoke-stained sill,*
*High up*
*Under a cloudy sky,*
*I saw a gray pigeon*
*(Inquisitive and shy)*
*Standing still*
*By my window,*
*And peeking into my room*
*On the sly …*

*Our eyes met and I heard the call and the cry*
*Of the wild and the free*
*Echoing through the stone-walled*
*Giant City,*
*Reminding me*
*Of a peaceful, simple world*
*In this restless place*
*Of confused complexity.*

64

# Sometime in July

The warm sunshine and the gentle breeze of summer has a magic quality. The smell of the fresh grass and the sweet fragrance of the blooming flowers cast upon us a magic spell. The world around us is suddenly filled with wonders.

I remember a sunny day in the month of July many years ago. I was sitting on a bench under a tall weeping willow with a picnic basket at my side, waiting for my husband, and my son and daughter, who were young children then, to return with a rented canoe. We planned to spend the afternoon pushing the smooth water of the lake with our wooden oars. As I looked aside, my eyes fell on a beautiful yellow water lily resting on a bed of soft, round, green leaves under the blue sky. It looked charming and innocent like a newly born infant. The hand of the years could never erase from my memory the love and the tenderness I felt for that slumbering lily.

Magda Herzberger

# The Lakeside

When the silence is broken
By cheers and laughter,
The sunshine looks brighter,
The water seems softer.

Empty boats and canoes
Are swaying,
Waiting for sailing.

In a side corner,
Humble and shy,
Wrapped in yellow ruffles,
Covered with droplets of dew,
And surrounded by a few
Tall weeping willows,
A lonely lily slumbers
On soft green, round pillows
Under the blue sky,

While the warm breeze
Of summer
Is humming an old lullaby.

# Part 2

# Contemplations

Past events, experiences, all kinds of feelings, fantasies, and daydreams are buried in the depth of our souls. But from time to time, they surface and manifest themselves in different forms in our various contemplative thoughts.

## Sanctuary

There is a free world of the spirit
Buried in the depth of the soul,
Where thoughts roam freely,
Where earthly barriers fall—
In this heavenly domain,
Mortal traits untouched remain—
In this mysterious realm,
Surrounded by beauty and calm,
The sparks of life live on and on,
Long after physical bodies are gone—

Magda Herzberger

# Search for My True Self

Where are you, my true self?
Did you get lost in the maze of destiny?
Did the passing years
Snatch you away from me?
I remember when you were at my side,
We walked together the city streets
And the countryside—
We were always a good team
And now, you appear only in my dream.

Why did you leave me behind?
Why were you so selfish and unkind?
Wherever you are,
No matter how far,
Please come and join me
On my life's terrain,
I want to be with you again—

At one point on my earthly station
I went through a great transformation—
And I noticed your absence,
I miss your presence—
You were always silent and reserved,
Content and undisturbed—
Did you ever miss my company?

70

# Midnight Musings

*You are a part of me,*
*My spiritual self—*
*Why do you ignore me*
*And place me on a shelf?*
*I hope to find you one day,*
*And then forever*
*With me you will stay—*

Magda Herzberger

# Invasion

Images of youth
From years passed by,
In the depth of your soul
Dormant they lie,
Until the day when suddenly
Upon you they call
And on the screens of memory
They start to roll—
You see yourself float
On the stream of life,
Witnessing your sweet joy
And your bitter strife—

They look like dreams
Projected on your spirit's screens,
Like beams of light
Appearing in the dark night,
Or like pieces of puzzles
Revealed and solved—
Mysteries and secrets
Kept by the self on hold,
Gradually unfold—

*Buried painful feelings and thoughts*
*Experienced but never told,*
*Become once more alive*
*And you wonder*
*If under their strong pressure*
*You can still survive—*

Magda Herzberger

# Introspection

On some black silent nights
Void of lights and sights,
I lay in my bed
And all kinds of thoughts
Turn around in my head.
Being unable to sleep,
I twist and turn
And start to weep.

I listen to the rhythmical ticking
Of my clock on the night table,
And to the cracking sounds
Of the wood structure
In our home,
And the spirits of past memories
Begin to roam in my mind.

I think of my youth
Which I left behind,
And I feel the grip of old age.
Gradually, I am locked
In the cage of reminiscences.
As my nostalgic mood
Intensifies and advances,
I fall into the pit of melancholy,

*Where all kinds of questions*
*Are haunting me.*

*Did I face bravely*
*The tribulations of my life?*
*Did I succeed in my strife?*
*Was I always true to myself?*

*As long as I was free to choose my way,*
*I can say that I didn't stray*
*From the right direction.*
*But there were times*
*When I was rendered helpless*
*And exposed to great distress,*
*By being pushed around forcefully*
*By the cruel hand of destiny,*
*Into the wild jungle*
*Of pain, suffering, and negativity.*

*Through the years I experienced*
*Love, peace, and harmony.*
*But I also was subjected*
*To the horrors of hatred,*
*Discrimination and cruelty,*
*During my captivity*
*In the concentration camps*
*Of Germany.*

# Magda Herzberger

By being a Jew,
I witnessed the ravages
Of World War II
And saw the victims of the Holocaust.
Therefore, this message I cast
Upon all the members of the new
And the old generation.

Try to enjoy life fully,
The best you can,
On your temporary life's station.
Have a positive attitude,
Let your heart be filled
With contentment and gratitude.
Thank the Almighty for bestowing upon you
The great gift of life.
Continue your daily strife.

Try to be active
As long as you are around.
You will have unlimited time
To rest and be immobile
When buried underground.

# Transformation

*Some day when ardent youth*
*Will leave your heart,*
*Don't let the joy of life*
*From you depart.*
*Let passion's flames still burn within*
*Your soul's abandoned silent inn,*
*To warm the space left behind,*
*Where happiness and peace*
*You still can find.*
*Don't be blind,*
*Look and discover*
*All the treasures of your mind.*

*Abandon dreams*
*Which can't come true.*
*Discard nostalgic yearnings,*
*Don't let them pierce you through.*
*Accept the changing world,*
*Welcome the altered you.*

*Light the candle of truth*
*And say goodbye with dignity to youth.*
*Go on with your life,*
*Make it anew!*
*And don't forget that Almighty God*
*Is watching over you.*

# Magda Herzberger

*Have faith in the Divine Spirit,*
*Let it elate your mental state.*
*It will give you strength and determination*
*To face the painful truth*
*With dignity and grace,*
*That nothing stays the same*
*On this earth's face.*
*And say goodbye without complaints,*
*With no tears to fleeing youth,*
*To the past years,*
*To their pleasures,*
*And lost treasures.*

*Keep in mind*
*That the Almighty is always at your side.*
*The Creator is your Protector*
*And your Guide.*
*Therefore, don't be afraid to walk*
*On the long corridor of life,*
*Don't ever give up your goals*
*And your strife.*

*Ignore the signs of old age,*
*Open a new page*
*In the book of life!*
*Be brave and strong,*
*Hope and believe*
*That nothing in your life*
*Can go wrong.*

# Thoughts in May

A positive frame of mind, regardless of our age, can do wonders for us by minimizing our worries and anxieties. It can increase our ability to cope with the everyday problems of life and the constant changes we face.

Pleasant thoughts develop our awareness of the beautiful world surrounding us and make us more considerate and responsive to our loved ones and to our fellow human beings. At the same time they give us inspiration and motivation to develop our inner resources, which in turn supply us with the spiritual strength necessary in order to create an eternal spring and summer in our hearts.

## Advice

*Don't succumb to the weeds of doom!*
*Be like a tree in bloom—*
*Enjoy life's precious hours,*
*Display your colorful flowers—*
*Let spring enter your heart,*
*Don't let your spirit fall apart.*
*Never be afraid of a fresh new start.*
*Let bright tomorrow*
*Lift your sorrow—*
*Circle the land of Joy and Freedom,*
*Cling to the wings of Love and Wisdom—*

Magda Herzberger

# Thoughts in September

The month of September is the escort of summer and the announcer of fall.

The life of the seasons is programmed and controlled by the Invisible Hands of the Creator. There is a designated and limited time for everything.

Our life cycles are also directed by the same Eternal Power. Birth, growth, maturation, and death are constantly alternating in the seasons of our existence.

We must yield at all times to the Will of Almighty God who created the universe and us.

## The Leaves of Life

*In the fall of my life*
*The yellow leaves of age*
*Are floating—*
*Disconnected from the trunk of the years.*
*Once they were fresh and green,*
*Nourished by the sap of youth.*
*Now, suspended in the air,*
*They wait in despair*
*To hit the ground of no return,*
*Succumbing to nature's ancient law*
*That reads:*

# Magda Herzberger

*You are born to grow and ripen.*
*When your mission is fulfilled,*
*You must yield*
*To the Creator's Will*
*And drop still.*
*From dust you emerged,*
*To ashes you return,*
*Eternity is only God's concern.*

# Practical Advice

As you walk on life's stage,
Regardless of your age,
Don't ask the rose in bloom
When its beauty will fade.
And never question death
If it intends to strike you soon
With its sharp blade.
Pass in silence
Through the fields and meadows,
Inhale the sweet fragrance
Of delicate flowers,
Enjoy your precious hours!

Taste the fresh drops
Of the morning dew,
It will renew your strength and vigor,
Protecting you from mental stupor.
Embrace on your way
The tall and friendly trees,
To find happiness and peace.
Be sure to greet the earth
And the grass under your feet.
They will be your cushions
And your mortal sheet,
When your heart ceases to beat.

Magda Herzberger

# Fantasies

On a distant island
In the midst of the vast sea,
I stand on the sandy beach
Of fantasy,
Listening to the waves'
Magic symphony—
My thoughts are far removed
From crude reality—
My eyes are immersed
In the beauty
Surrounding me—

No human souls are here around,
Only me, the soft ground,
And the sea—
I feel happy and free,
Liberated from worry
And anxiety—
I gently sing in harmony
With the loud chorus of the sea—

A strange ethereal voice
Emerges from nowhere
And echoes in the air—

"Come to me,
Let's be together
From now till forever"—

I succumb to this haunting constant call,
And jump into the sea,
Offering my body and soul,
Submersing into the deep bottom
Of eternity—

There are no sounds here anymore,
I can't see the distant shore.
I am now a part of the sea,
And will remain its constant company—

I renounced all earthly pleasures,
Ambitions and glory—
I found peace and harmony
And answered the question,
To be or not to be.

And now it is for you to decide
On the other side,
If I was right or wrong,
Weak or strong—
Or, just a dreamer
On a beautiful day
In summer.

Magda Herzberger

# Contemplations in November

Looking at the bare branches of an old maple tree, the principles of strength, endurance, faith, hope, and bravery were instantly revealed to me.

## Resiliency

*Old maple tree,*
*All your golden leaves are gone—*
*Only your gray skeleton*
*Is bathing in the sun—*
*Fall stripped your emerald crown,*
*Leaving you naked and dull,*
*Exposing your bare skull—*
*But, within your roots,*
*Life pulsates without cease—*
*Strange forces release*
*Your vital sap of life—*

*Your wrinkled weather-beaten trunk*
*Is strong and brave,*
*Keeping you away from the grave—*

# Magda Herzberger

*On cold and snowy winter days*
*When howling winds pass through,*
*You take your beauty sleep,*
*Making yourself anew—*
*When spring strikes its gentle strings,*
*You wake up from your dreams,*
*Greeting with joy*
*The melting lakes and streams—*
*You witness the birth of fresh buds*
*On your wooded arms,*
*Displaying with pride your leafy palms—*

*Old maple tree,*
*My dear friend,*
*Lend me your dignity,*
*Your strength, your courage*
*And your flexibility.*

# Regeneration

There was once upon a time a magic tree
Called Majesty,
Whose noble children were
The golden leaves of Peace and
Harmony.
One day the raging storm
Of hate and cruelty
Was on its way to destroy Majesty.
The evil winds of envy and jealousy
Were pounding on Serenity and Beauty.
All the golden leaves of
Peace and Harmony
Were torn apart.
The wicked brutal forces
Wanted to break Majesty's gentle heart.

But, they were beating
The impenetrable golden trunk in vain,
Entrance to its sacred core
They could not gain.
The sap of life was still flowing within.
To kill the tree of Love and Life
Would be a mighty sin.
The white angels of Peace
Were looking down in awe
At the stripped naked crown.

# Magda Herzberger

God descended from His High Throne
And declared that new golden leaves
Of Harmony and Peace
Will instantly be born.

A great miracle took place
On God's command,
A mystery, no one could ever understand.
New shoots of Serenity started to show
And the fruits of Love began to grow.
The Creator's Power knows no limit,
He holds the seeds of Body and Spirit.

# Life Cycles

*Where are the flowers of yesterday?*
*The frost came and took their beauty away.*
*It was cruel and unkind*
*To leave only the shriveled petals and stems behind.*
*But, the roots are still alive*
*Buried deeply underground,*
*Giving birth to new shoots,*
*When Spring comes around.*

*The same cycle is repeated year after year—*
*Some flowers fall into their eternal sleep,*
*But, in their place new ones appear.*
*We humans also meet a similar fate—*
*We bloom for awhile,*
*And then gradually we disintegrate.*
*Generations come and go,*
*Life is moving to and fro.*

Magda Herzberger

# Thoughts in November

The beautiful season of fall comes to an end in the month of November. The gusty cold winds remove the golden, rusty leaves from their supporting branches and hurl them to the ground, where they pile up in dead heaps.

The icy hands of the frost strip the pale petals of the ailing, frail flowers. Dry brown patches blemish the green face of the earth. Only the evergreens are untouched, still displaying their beauty.

The melancholic and nostalgic mood of autumn is conducive to reflection. It reminds us of our temporary stay on this earth. It points out that nothing stays forever. There is a time to be born and a time to say goodbye to life and youth. It brings us home to the eternal truth that we are but mortals governed by a Higher Power, and we have only limited control over our destiny.

## Miracle Worker

*The falling leaves cover the ground*
*As autumn's face appears—*
*The lonely trees shed their bitter tears,*
*Mourning the passing of the years—*
*Winter's white hands reach out*
*To grasp the frail body of fall—*

# Magda Herzberger

*The loud call of icy winds is heard,*
*There is no trace of a butterfly*
*Or a singing bird—*
*Dark clouds circle the sky,*
*The sad sigh of the weary earth*
*Echoes in the air,*
*As marigolds, petunias, and dahlias*
*Slowly die in despair—*

*Life is moving to and fro,*
*Seasons come and go—*
*Who is the master who controls*
*The universe and us?*
*Who created mankind and the sod?*
*The everlasting power of Almighty God—*

# Patterns of Destiny

Piles of rusty golden leaves,
Brittle and dry, destined to die,
Lie limp on the freezing ground, everywhere,
While many of their kind, left behind,
Still float around in the air, in awe and despair—
Stripped of their supporting limbs,
They are twisted and curled,
Pushed, tossed, twirled and hurled
To the earth's pale face,
By the cruel gusty winds of fall—

As they land, some gently roll with grace,
On the wilted surface of the grass—
Others run and race en masse,
On the pavements of every street—
There are those which leap and hop
And dance without a stop,
To the fast beat of autumn's drum,
While the desolate bare trees hum
Their melancholic melodies—
Rooted in earth, they helplessly stand—
Their robbed branches squeak and bend,
As icy winds blow through their naked bodies—

# Magda Herzberger

Their weary limbs will soon hang low,
Under the weight of the approaching
Winter's heavy snow—
Their survival will be at stake,
Some of them will break—
But they must bear with dignity,
Their assigned destiny—
They must abide by nature's ancient
In-built laws and rules—
There are no magic hands or tools
Which can alter the course and shape
Of God's creation—
The power of the Almighty is limitless,
Beyond our reach, or imagination—

As the years come and go,
We humans are also moving to and fro—
There are four seasons in each person's life,
Birth, maturation, old age, and cessation—
There is a time when we begin,
And a time when we end our strife—
So often we ask the question, why?
But we can never get a clear reply—
So life goes on and on,
Meanwhile we have our tears and fun.
There is nothing new under the sun—
There is a constant repetition
Of Mankind's mission and fate—

*There is no end to our debate*
*Whether all these properties and laws*
*Are right or wrong or fair—*

*But, we really shouldn't care,*
*Because we can't halt anyway*
*The designated stages of transformations*
*Occurring on our predestined way—*
*And it is beyond our ability*
*To change, or rearrange*
*The distinct patterns of destiny—*
*We can't stop death or old age,*
*Neither can we prevent a storm's fury or rage—*
*Certain things we can't control,*
*Sooner or later, for all of us, the bell will toll—*

*Peace of mind we never find—*
*We live constantly with insecurity,*
*With confusion and perplexity.*
*Nevertheless, it is still worthwhile*
*To persist to exist,*
*To be around above the ground,*
*To tend to our daily tasks—*
*To enjoy life fully as long as it lasts,*
*To fulfill our dreams and goals,*
*Regardless of what destiny casts*
*Upon our bodies and souls.*

Magda Herzberger

# Daydreams

In the world of reality,
I am bound to earth's gravity.
But, in the realm of fantasy,
I am boundless and free,
Nothing is barred from me—
I can be anywhere,
And become anything
I want to be—
I can be the mountain,
The earth, the sea,
Or, any part of the distant galaxy—

I can become a shining star,
Or, sit on the moon—
I can turn into a gentle breeze
Or, a raging typhoon—
I can cross on foot the ocean
Or, be transformed
Into love's magic potion—
I can play the role of a sage
With a saintly visage—

I can be a rich and beautiful princess
Adored and feared—
Or, a wise prophet
With a long white beard—

*Or, a genius, mystical,*
*Eccentric and weird—*
*I can be an adventurer,*
*Exploring the wild—*
*Or, a conformist, reserved and mild,*
*Or, a writer, skillful with words*
*And fast with a pen,*
*Whose stories and verse*
*Echo through the universe—*

*I can turn into a tree,*
*Be bound again, not free—*
*And if I wish*
*I can twitch my eye*
*And become a witch*
*In the middle ages,*
*Fulfilling my wildest desire,*
*Without being set on fire—*
*I can retain my youth and beauty*
*Through life's many stages—*
*I can attain anything I want easily*
*Without any effort or difficulty—*

*But, one thing I never want to be,*
*The representative of war, hatred,*
*Prejudice and cruelty—*

# Magda Herzberger

*I would rather be an angel*
*Sent from above,*
*To bring humanity*
*The sacred gift of love—*

*Daydreams are delightful and pleasant,*
*But, we still have to deal and live*
*With the problems and hardships*
*Of the present—*
*We can debate*
*Whether daydreams are detrimental*
*To our mental state,*
*Or, if they threaten*
*The safety of our sanity,*
*By getting us*
*Out of touch with reality—*

*Some people say,*
*If we practice them each day,*
*We can lose our way,*
*Ending up perplexed and confused—*
*Our judgment might be altered,*
*Becoming poor and diffused,*
*By living in castles in the air*
*From which we can fall through,*
*In awe and despair,*

*And get injured*
*From landing abruptly,*
*On the rough hard ground*
*Of the real world—*
*Maybe to some*
*All these misfortunes*
*Might have occurred—*

*Yet, I don't care what anyone says,*
*All I know is that there are*
*Many different approaches and ways*
*To cope with the burden*
*Of the present days—*
*I believe that it is beneficial,*
*Healthy and good,*
*To ingest occasionally*
*Some magical, spiritual food*
*And to seek a peaceful,*
*Pleasurable refuge*
*From worries' deluge—*
*Besides, impossible dreams*
*Sometimes can come true—*
*This is a little secret*
*Between me and you.*

Magda Herzberger

# Strange Friendship

I touched the palms
Of the tall blue spruce
For many years—
A strong friendship was sealed
Between me and the green giant.
A tree can be such a true companion,
So patient, so reliant.

I ran to it
When tears ran down my cheeks,
I sat underneath its shadow
When it was time for dreams.
I rushed to it
With a joyful laughter,
I crawled to it
When my spirits were low,
Feeling empty and shallow.

Is there any good reason
Why a tree and me
Shouldn't be friends
And silently,
Without ever exchanging a word,
Hold hands?

# Eyewitness

It was the end of November. The raging, icy winds of autumn were beheading the pale, freezing flowers and were stripping the discolored brittle leaves from their supporting branches. Our old, hard maple tree was robbed of its garment, standing naked and lonely. Its yellow, rusty leaves were lying in dead heaps around its solid base. I stood by the thick, wrinkled, grieving trunk, looking with sadness at the ravages of fall. Then, my eyes followed the bare crown depleted of its ornaments. To my surprise, I detected a single leaf still clinging to its naked twig. It was also doomed to perish sooner or later. It looked so desolate and pitiful on its deathbed. All its friends were gone. There was no one to give comfort or companionship.

I felt great compassion and at the same time, also admiration, for this last leaf, still hanging on to its life source for three more weeks. I watched its brave struggle day by day.

The desire to preserve the memory and the strife of this brave leaf prompted me to write the following poem.

Magda Herzberger

# Isolation

Like a lost penny
After a theft,
A single leaf
On the robbed branches
Is left.

There it lingers
Amidst curled wood fingers,
As the rain sprinkles
The dry wrinkles
Of the bark.

And in the spark
Of the lightning,
It is frightening and sad
To look at the last leaf
On its deathbed.

# Season's Greetings

December is a special month of the year filled with the joy and excitement of the holiday season. It is a busy time. The streets and the shops are crowded with people looking for Christmas gifts and decorations. The children reveal their hearts' secret desires to the kind and jolly Santa Claus, hoping that their wishes will come true. Families get together to commemorate the birth of Christ. They are feasting, rejoicing, singing hymns of praise, and exchanging presents with their loved ones.

December also marks the beginning of another season, a festive time in the life of nature when winter sings its haunting, melancholic melody to the rusty brown grass and to the gray, naked, forsaken trees. Countless, tiny frozen stars fall silently upon the weary, discolored earth covered with ice, giving birth to winter's crystal paradise of solitude. Above the wonderland of hard frost and soft, white, pure, fresh snow, the harps of heaven are played by the invisible hands of the Creator.

The celestial music contains a soothing balm, bringing peace, serenity and calm.

Magda Herzberger

# Hidden Wonders

Piles of snow
Across the street
And screeching ice
Under my feet,
Cold and sleet—

A winter world
In which no singing bird
Is heard,
No green foliage
Upon the weary trees,
No buzzing of the bees,
No bending flowers,
No warm breeze—

Only sparkling, countless stars
And bars of music
Mixed with flats and sharps,
Float from unseen harps,
To form the interlude
Of silent solitude—

# Thoughts in February

Many people don't look forward to the cold winter months when icy winds are howling and the hard-crusted earth is covered with a white mantle ornamented with frozen stars. But I am very fond of this special season. Each of its months is connected with an important and meaningful event. December commemorates the birth of Christ; January ushers in the New Year; and February marks my birthday.

I admire the magnificent beauty and the quiet, dignified, solitary spirit of winter. Its pure, soft snow reflects peace and serenity. It provides a soothing balm for our wounds and a cure for the ills of mankind. I have seen the ravages and the destruction caused by war. My plea to winter is to bring peace and to purify the battered earth from bloodshed. May brotherhood and love descend upon our planet.

# I Saw Them All

*I saw the flags*
*Of mortal sin*
*Wherever I have been—*
*I saw the flood*
*Of human blood*
*Rising on the green—*

# Magda Herzberger

*I saw the flag*
*Of victory*
*Shining in the sun—*
*I saw the graves*
*Of all of those*
*Who eternally*
*Were gone—*

# Plea for Peace

*Come, winter,*
*With your ice and snow,*
*Spread your white blanket*
*Wherever you go—*
*Cover the shivering grass,*
*The naked branches,*
*Fill the abandoned trenches.*
*Bring peace, silence, purity—*
*Don't let blood stain*
*The weary, battered earth,*
*Give birth to friendship,*
*Love, and Unity.*

Magda Herzberger

# On the Wings of Inspiration

The following group of poems illustrates the great variety of messages that come to me from my Miraculous Muse. The poem below tells the story of her arrival in my life.

## Strange Visitor

*The Spirit of Poetry*
*Came to me*
*Long ago,*
*To reveal the many wonders*
*Of the mind,*
*Helping me to find*
*The road to eternity ...*

*At our first encounter*
*I was distrustful,*
*Encompassed by fear,*
*Bewildered and shy,*
*Pondering why*
*Did this mysterious specter*
*Suddenly appear,*
*Like an angel*
*Sent from the sky ...*

# Magda Herzberger

*Since then,*
*My life has never been the same …*
*Strange apparition,*
*I know your name,*
*Miraculous Muse!*

*You opened my heart,*
*Planting into it*
*The magic seeds of inspiration …*
*You penetrated my spirit*
*Starting its revolution,*
*Bringing forth new thoughts*
*And evolution …*

*Who sent to me*
*This friend of my soul*
*Who guides my thoughts*
*And leads the path of truth,*
*Who holds within*
*Her mystic shrine*
*The sacred power*
*Of youth?*

# Self-Projection

In the empty space of loneliness
I drift along
With thoughts detached
From daily tasks
And feelings dulled.
I am slowly lulled
Into drowsiness.
In the stillness
Of the night,
As I close my sleepy eyes
Ready for the day's repose,
I see the image of myself
As an old friend
Who never really changed.

I see the child,
The young adult,
The middle-aged,
Mingled in a familiar face,
Smiling at me
And reminding me
Who I am.
So far I've come
From my first day of life
And yet, the spark which started then
Is still here,
Shining in the dark.

Magda Herzberger

# Maturity

My thoughts wander
On the fields of memory,
Searching for the Tree of Remembrance,
Under which are buried the fragments
Of my childhood and adolescence.
My adulthood is also resting
Under its wrinkled trunk.

My youth is gone,
Old age took its place.
I have to accept it with grace
And live my life the best I can
At this stage.
I must open a new chapter
Of my existence.

I must stop my resistance
To something new,
Which grew out of the old—
"Be flexible and strong"
I was told,
"To feel sorry for yourself
Is very wrong."

# Magda Herzberger

# Loyalty

The children of my mind
Are very precious to me.
They never ask for anything,
They are my faithful company.
They are my joys in time of awe
And my shield against sorrow.
They are the hopes of tomorrow.
They are like fresh mountain streams
Nourishing my happy dreams.

# Just Matter Without a Soul

As time goes slowly on,
Gradually I become a piece of stone,
Too heavy for the wind to blow me away,
Burden to the soil, standing in its way.

Then, suddenly one day,
I am lifted up and carried away.
I am rolling, twisting, twirling, swirling,
All along my way,
Nothing can stop me on this terrible day!

Where is the place of my destination?
Will I live there in complete isolation?
I wish I could stop
And rest peacefully on some lonely spot.

I am falling, falling! Oh, what a shock!
Then, a sudden unexpected stop.
I am still in one piece! I didn't break!
But where am I, for heaven's sake?

I look around ...
I see I have reached my destination.
Here I will rest in eternal desolation.

# Magda Herzberger

*A piece of stone, nothing more,*
*Lying still on the bottom*
*Of the vast ocean floor.*
*Here I will stay*
*Till the end of my last day.*
*Just matter,*
*Without shape, without body, without soul,*
*Forgotten forever by all.*

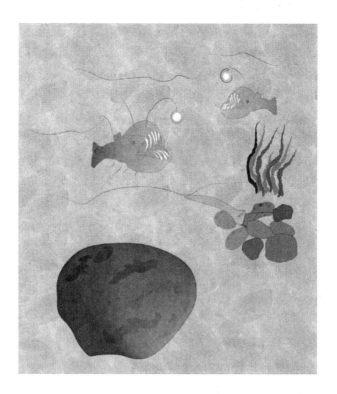

# The Hand of Destiny

"Little bee, little bee,
Come to me!
My nectar will give you
The finest honey."

"Sweet daisy,
I am in a hurry today,
But I will come to you
On some other day."

"Little bee," said the daisy,
"I feel so sad and lonely.
Please keep me company.
Your presence will make me so happy.
Tomorrow I might not be here anymore.
My petals will shrivel and fall.
Therefore, please listen to my call And
ease the sorrow of my soul."

The blooming daisy was so beautiful,
Fresh and lovely.
The little bee started thinking
Of flawless honey.
He fell under the power
Of the charming flower

*And decided to keep her company,*
*But only for half an hour.*

*After that he said:*
*"Now I must go,*
*But I will see you tomorrow,*
*And we will spend more time together*
*No matter what would be*
*The weather!"*

*Early the following morning,*
*The little bee was eagerly looking*
*For the lovely daisy.*
*But she was gone.*
*He found her lifeless body*
*Under the bright sun.*
*The wild winds blowing through the night*
*Had crushed her head,*
*And she laid still*
*On her deathbed.*

*"Sweet little daisy,"*
*Cried the little bee,*
*"Why did you desert me?*
*I feel so sad and lonely,*
*And so sorry and guilty,*
*That I didn't stay with you*
*Longer yesterday.*

*And now, death has taken you away from me.*
*But I could not foresee*
*That the cruel hand of fate*
*Would slam on you death's gate,*
*And cast upon me*
*So much pain and misery.*
*I miss so much your company!*
*My sweet little daisy,*
*Rest peacefully."*

Magda Herzberger

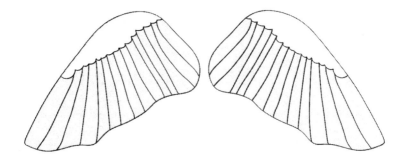

# On the Wings of Fantasy

When the enchanting delicate fragrance
Of blooming flowers fills my nostrils,
The thrills of joy engulf me,
Casting a magic spell
Upon my soul and body.
They dispel the dark clouds
Of worry and anxiety,
And suddenly I perceive the beauty
Of the world surrounding me.

I start looking around
And I discover the green grass
Covering the ground.
My eyes follow the magnificent big trees,
Loaded with luscious fresh leaves.
I listen to the buzzing of the bees,
To the songbirds' happy tunes,
And to the robin's call.

And I look at a squirrel running fearlessly
On the tip of the high electrical pole.
I also notice the intricate patterns
Of the spider's web,
Woven from a special silky thread,
And I see a fly ensnared inside,
Destined for the fatal stab.

# Magda Herzberger

*I look up to the blue sky*
*With a happy smile on my face.*
*I say my thanks and grace to God*
*For being healthy and alive,*
*And for the Almighty's constant guide.*
*I am just a running passerby*
*On life's rough terrain,*
*Created by the Supreme Sovereign.*

# Advice to the Housewife

If you are smart,
Sometimes stop your work
Before you start!
Let the dishes pile up,
Leave beds undone,
Relax and have fun!
Put aside your dust cloth
And your broom,
Leave the kitchen
And your room.

Get into your car
And drive away far.
Have a nice ride,
Enjoy the countryside.
Take a break
For your health's sake.
Change your behavior
And you will feel great
And superior.

But if you are one of those
With a strong compulsion
To work without repose,
I have for you a good solution.

# Magda Herzberger

Hire a helper and let her do
All the chores for you;
The dishes, the beds,
The scrubbing, washing, cleaning,
Pressing, knitting, sewing and mending.
It is very healthy
To stay away occasionally
From your daily monotony,
And leave your job undone.

It will not hurt anyone
If your work will be done
By someone while you are gone.
Delegate your duty temporarily
To somebody or to none,
And set yourself free
From the dark hues
Of the housewife's blues.

# A Song Is Born

*My harp lies still*
*Waiting for swift fingers*
*And melodies to fill—*
*There in the corner*
*Behind the rocking chair.*

*It longs to be taken out*
*Into the fresh air—*
*Where the rabbits sleep,*
*Sheltered in their lair,*
*Where the birds sing*
*Their songs of spring and summer,*
*Where the woodpeckers hammer.*

*When nature's sounds*
*Are put together,*
*A song is born*
*On the strings of my harp—*
*And thus is recorded*
*The song of the lark,*
*The whisper of the grass,*
*The whistle of the wind,*
*The bouncing of raindrops*
*Hitting the treetops,*
*The strong beat*
*Of heaven's drummer,*

Magda Herzberger

*The breath of spring,*
*The pulse of summer.*

*Come, my harp,*
*Let's go outside.*
*This room is small,*
*The world is wide—*

# Compensation

Is there anyone
Who scorns the rose
Because of its thorns?
Or, would you say
That it is less of a flower
Than a tulip born in May?
The sweet, delicate fragrance
Of a rose
Softens the sharpness of its stem
Making it love's symbolic diadem.

Magda Herzberger

# On Wings of Wisdom

In a distant mountain's heart,
Within a cave deprived of light,
Far away and out of sight,
Sits a Saint with folded knees,
Motionless and with closed eyes,
Entranced in Spirit's Paradise—
There is no trace of sadness
On his finely chiseled face,
He looks content and peaceful
In his silent, stony dwelling place—

Through the windows of his soul,
He sees man's world out of control,
And perceives his own main goal—

Enveloped in his deep meditation
At his remote, solitary station,
Enclosed in total isolation,
The sacred port of Paradise he is seeing—
A better world comes into being,
He hears the angels sing,
He feels the peace that faith can bring.

He responds to God's revelation
With a feeling of joyful elation.
His spirit soars
To Heaven's door
On wings of wisdom
Now and forevermore.

# Separate Entities

Look for a star,
Call it your own—
It will be yours
Only till dawn—

Search for an ideal,
Call it your star—
It will shine day and night
Wherever you are—

Magda Herzberger

# Life Counseling

*The song of youth*
*Echoes in the air,*
*While the old and feeble*
*Struggle in despair,*
*Clinging to life's last straw,*
*Refusing to let it go.*
*We live only once,*
*And for such a short term.*
*Yet, most of the time,*
*We are grim and stern!*

*Why don't we learn*
*That hearty laughter,*
*A kind smile,*
*And the warm glow of love*
*Were given for use*
*To each of us*
*From above?*
*So often we take for granted*
*Such precious gifts as these.*

*Slow down your frantic pace,*
*Stop for a minute, please!*
*And think before it is too late.*

*Try to change for the better*
*Your mental state,*
*Before you are struck*
*By the forceful hand of Fate.*
*Don't be, throughout life,*
*Just a passerby,*
*But be a participant*
*Of the earth, sea, and sky,*
*And share your heart*
*With humanity.*
*Have compassion, affection,*
*Concern, and pity*
*For your fellowman*
*Whenever you can.*

*Cherish and respect*
*The great gifts of life:*
*Faith, Hope, and Love*
*And lift your spirit*
*To the distant*
*Infinite galaxy above!*

Magda Herzberger

# Call for Breakfast

*Written for my son in 1963*

The morning light
Shines so bright,
Open your eyes,
Look at the sun,
The night is gone—
Wake up, my dear son!

Don't linger long
In your soft, warm bed.
Come and eat
Your breakfast instead.
Don't let the day pass
In hours of sleep!
Creep out of your blanket
And pillow,
And greet by the window
The old weeping willow.

Hurry up,
Don't be so slow!
Wake up, my son,
Before the day is gone!

# Reverie

*A young girl*
*Wrapped in a white veil*
*Was pacing slowly*
*The narrow forest trail.*
*Her body was slender and frail,*
*Her cheeks were hollow and pale,*
*Her eyes had the glitter*
*Of diamond and silver.*
*She was singing the song*
*Of a lonely nightingale—*

*"Come to my nest*
*To my small shadow,*
*Follow the trees*
*And the green meadow.*
*Hold out your palm,*
*I will come to you,*
*Happy and calm.*
*Extend your arm*
*But, please do me no harm.*
*Caress with your soft fingers*
*My bright, light feathers,*
*And I will sing to you*
*The song of lovers:*

# Magda Herzberger

*"Kiss me,*
*And hold me tight,*
*Under the yellow moon's*
*Golden light.*
*Come with me*
*And listen*
*To the sound of the forest.*
*Come and rest*
*On the green velvet,*
*And dream*
*From sunset*
*Til morning.*
*Take this ring,*
*Slide it on your finger,*
*I am yours,*
*You are mine, forever."*

*Shadows and echoes*
*Of lovers and heroes,*
*Cupid's old arrows,*
*Phantoms and mirages*
*Of fools and sages*
*From different ages,*
*Moving images*
*Of past passages*
*Fill up the forest—*

*A lonely girl,*
*Barefoot and shabby*
*But cheerful and happy,*
*Listens and dreams*
*As she follows*
*The path between two hills,*
*Collecting berries*
*And wild cherries,*
*While the twilight steals*
*The bright rays*
*Of the sun.*
*Her house is in the valley down.*
*She walks like a queen*
*Without a crown—*

Magda Herzberger

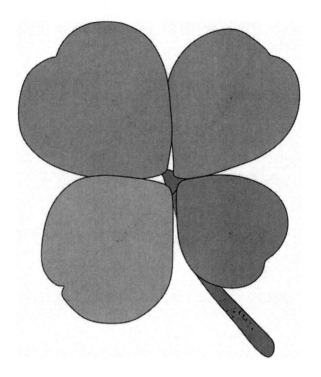

# Symbol of Luck

I looked for the four-leafed clover
All over the fields,
The rusty meadows,
Passing and crossing
The golden shadows—
I trespassed the dry brown grass
And trod the leaf-embedded earth—

I ran over the green hills
Searching among
The dancing daffodils,
Between the lines
Of yellow dandelions,
And amidst the violets, tulips,
Roses, and asters,
Until my feet were covered
With blisters—

As I looked around
Behind the black-eyed Susans
And the goldenrod,
I found the symbol of luck
On the ground,
Stuck in the road—

# Magda Herzberger

I bent down to pick it up
But then it started to hop and hop
From place to place,
Mocking me,
And laughing straight into my face—
I tried to catch it, in vain,
Chasing it to the  edge of  the brook—
 But before I could utter, "Look!"
The four tiny leaves were gone—

I was alone in the silent park
Looking at the shining sun
And facing the wrinkled tree bark—
Next to me,
Hidden in the dewy grass,
Was the four-leafed clover—
My dream was over.

# Trip to Paradise

On a dark night
When the stars and the moon
Were out of sight,
The Muse appeared to me
Clad in the white robe
Of innocence and purity,
Looking like an angel
Sent from Heaven
To brighten my barren spirit.

The candle of hope
In my heart was lighted,
The flames of fantasy ignited.
I left my dark room,
The dwelling place
Of oppressive gloom.
And I was soaring the heights
In the middle of the night,
With utmost delight,
My house was out of sight.

I passed the traveling clouds
Drifting in the atmosphere
With great skill and care,

# Magda Herzberger

*Leaving behind the earth's hard crust,*
*Its dust and warm core,*
*Reaching Heaven's golden door.*

*And I entered the Garden of Eden*
*Where Adam and Eve were born.*
*The gate of the ancient magical Haven*
*Was torn.*
*The place was deserted and bare.*
*No one could remain*
*On this sacred abandoned terrain,*
*Where the first humans*
*Were chased away and punished forever*
*By the Creator.*

*It was painful to walk*
*On the rough, prickly path*
*In the place of God's anger and wrath.*
*There was no one there with whom to talk.*
*I was strolling along*
*On the ground where I didn't belong,*
*Destined only for a heavenly throng.*

*Suddenly the silhouettes*
*Of a man and a woman,*
*A ghostly couple,*
*Appeared at my side.*
*They were wearing garments of leaves,*
*Serving as briefs.*

142

*I heard them say:*

*"We are the spirits*
*Of Adam and Eve,*
*This place we must leave.*
*We are still chased, admonished,*
*And gravely punished*
*By the Creator*
*For tasting the fruit of knowledge.*
*We must run forever*
*From place to place.*
*We are still cast out of God's grace*
*And deprived of a resting place.*

*Stranger, go away!*
*In this sacred place*
*You can't stay.*
*You don't belong here.*
*The judgment of God*
*For your intrusion*
*You should fear."*

*The very first humans*
*Passed me by,*
*Waving to me, "Goodbye,"*
*And then they flew up high,*
*Crossing the blue sky.*

# Magda Herzberger

*Then all at once,*
*All these heavenly visions disappeared,*
*And the vague contours*
*Of my room appeared.*
*Someone near*
*Whispered in my ear:*

*"Wake up from your deep sleep, my dear.*
*The night and your dream world are gone.*
*Come, and greet the rising sun.*
*Get up and hold my hand."*

*It was the soothing voice*
*O my beloved husband.*

# Awakening

*The sun pops out*
*Beyond the hills,*
*As the morning steals*
*The veil of the night.*
*Yesterday is sealed and gone.*
*The new day is born*
*Shining and bright.*

*The world of dreams*
*Vanished into nothingness,*
*As the light vanquished*
*The night of darkness.*

*What is ahead*
*We do not know.*
*Each new beginning*
*Is always a mystery,*
*Holding different things*
*For you and me.*

*Will it be happiness or sorrow?*
*Failure or success?*
*Death or a new breath?*
*All these are the secrets of tomorrow.*

# Magda Herzberger

*But now, look out the window,*
*See the virgin white, untouched,*
*Freshly fallen snow.*

*Watch the evergreens,*
*Ornamented with winter's stars,*
*Standing in a straight row,*
*And behold the gray silhouettes*
*Of the naked, leafless trees,*
*Loaded with winter's crystals,*
*Sparkling like precious stones.*

*Let your eyes follow*
*Winter's blinding glow*
*And the beauty of the universe.*
*Let your soul immerse*
*In God's wonderful creation,*
*And sense the intense*
*Peace and silence*
*Descending upon you*
*On your earthly station.*
*Enjoy the present and have fun,*
*Because the future is uncertain*
*And unknown.*

# On the Wings of Imagination

*I float above land and sea—*
*My thoughts are carrying me far away*
*To the world where I can't stay.*
*There is no landing place*
*High up in space—*
*I drift along day by day*
*And in my isolation*
*I dream about the art of creation.*

*As I circle above,*
*I see the flames of a burning love*
*Which cries for help,*
*Deafening my ears,*
*And helplessly*
*I burst into tears.*
*My heart feels dulled*
*And into melancholy*
*I am slowly lulled—*

*I hear the sound of the harp*
*And I see fingers touching the strings—*
*I listen to an old song*
*Which still clings,*
*To my memory—*

# Magda Herzberger

"Whisper to the wind,
Sing to the flowers,
Speak to the trees,
And tell about the treasures
Which the eye sees.
Listen to the song of life,
Think of the ultimate fate of man,
And try to live
The best you can—"

# Part 3

# A Glimpse into Life

Life is a mystery, a miracle created by Almighty God. Life is beautiful, but also changeable and unpredictable. The rhythm of life's pulse is controlled and directed by the invisible hands of The Creator.

Our fate and existence is predestined by The Ruler of Man and the Universe. Our mortal eyes can't see the unpaved road of the future.

## Mystery

*Somewhere, at the edge of nowhere,*
*Upon the unpaved road of the future,*
*The silhouette of my fate is projected—*
*But my mortal eyes can't see*
*The shape of my destiny—*
*Nor can my spirit grasp*
*Life's unpredictable course of action—*
*Only my striving body*
*Feels the agony of pain*
*And the joy of resurrection—*
*I am but a wave*
*In the ocean of existence,*
*Driven by the current of my thoughts*
*And protected by God's assistance—*

Magda Herzberger

# Uncertainty

No one can foretell
When for us will toll the bell,
Or what kind of events
Our fate will bring
Through summer, fall,
Winter and spring—
We have no control
Over our life-span,
Therefore we should live
The best we can—

Our destiny is in the hands
Of the Almighty—
To our Creator we should pray
To send us good luck,
Good health and happiness our way,
To grant us many years of life,
To assist us in our daily strife,
To help us to achieve
Our desired dreams and goals,
Before the bell for us tolls.

# Evoking the Muse

*Spirit of poetry,*
*Wherever you may be,*
*Listen to the melody*
*Of our time—*
*Come and dance with me*
*To the rhythm of the rhyme—*
*Let your light shine,*
*Lead me and teach me*
*To follow your line—*
*Leave behind*
*Your ancient bard*
*For whom, for many years*
*You stood on guard—*
*Don't let me wait too long,*
*Come, and let's create*
*A new song.*

Magda Herzberger

# Song of the Bard

*Someday you will understand*
*That I belong to "No Man's Land"*
*Where the Spirit is the King,*
*Where, embraced by the soul's*
*Eternal Spring,*
*The song of life I sing:*

*"Leave behind*
*Your futile thoughts—*
*Come with me to*
*The green hills of fantasy—*
*There, you will find*
*The hidden treasures*
*Of your mind*
*And the magic key*
*To the door*
*Of imagination —*

*"Unlock the wonders*
*Of creation,*
*To see life's beauty,*
*To reveal its mystery,*
*To discover man's*
*True mission and destiny—*

Then, pick up your pen
And write the "Songs of Life"
To humanity
The best you can."

Magda Herzberger

# Songs of Life

My soul is a captive of time,
My body to dust belongs.
My spirit is free
Creating my songs.
And if one day
Their melody finds its way
To your ears,
Hum it gently
And it will add color
To your faded years.
Let its sound echo
Through your heart.
By then, I may rest
Deep in the ground,
But my spirit
Will still follow you around.

# Summary

*A breath*
*A thought*
*A body caught*
*In life's web*
*Is me.*

*To feel*
*To be*
*And then to see*
*The face of death*
*Is my destiny.*

Magda Herzberger

# Farewell

*Someday*
*We will have to turn away*
*From life,*
*Stop our strife,*
*And leave behind*
*All the beauty we did find.*
*And say goodbye*
*To all the earthly things,*
*To the sun, to the starry sky—*
*Dark night will prevail*
*At the end of our trail,*
*Where death will hail*
*Its victory—*
*Forgotten we will be.*

*But, the trees above*
*Will still go on*
*Providing shade, protection, consolation*
*To the other generation.*
*And the open prairie*
*Will still be the place*
*Where the restless souls will roam,*
*Searching for fulfillments and goals,*
*While the grave will become*
*Our eternal, silent, somber home.*

# Wanderer

*Die not with tears,*
*With moans, or cries,*
*But with dignity and grace.*
*Engrave on the carved stone*
*Marking your resting place:*

*"Here lies my body,*
*Stripped of life,*
*Sold to earth*
*At a cheap price.*
*If you will ask*
*My spirit to rise,*
*You may discover,*
*To your surprise,*
*That it left long ago*
*With a small bundle of verse,*
*To roam forever*
*The eternal universe."*

Magda Herzberger

# Unanswered Questions

Many years of my life passed by so fast,
I can't tell which of the remaining ones
Will be my last—
I can't foresee
What the future holds for me—
Therefore, I intend to enjoy each day
The best I can,
Pretending that my life just recently began—
To the Almighty I pray,
Asking Him to send good health
And happiness my way,
During my limited stay on this earth—

I beseech the Lord
To help me give birth
To true music and verse,
And to teach me to understand
The mystery of the universe—

As long as my spirit maintains its youth
At this stage of my advanced age,
I can face the truth
And accept the gradual loss
Of my corporal and facial beauty.

I yearn only for longevity and creativity!
As long as I can think clearly
And create a wonder world of imagination,
Feeling the exhilarating sensation
Of being alive, useful, filled with energy,
And having my family at my side,
I am willing to part with my vanity and pride—

Some gray hair and wrinkles
Which I accumulate gradually
Don't bother me.
I am not unhappy or perturbed,
As long as the beauty of my soul is well preserved—

What can I leave behind
For mankind?
It seems only my thoughts put to words,
Which contain memories
From my life's scenes,
Passages of philosophy,
The contents of my dreams,
Descriptions of love, joy, agony,
And my musical scores of life's symphony—

Where will all these writings
And compositions land ultimately
After my life's cessation?

# Magda Herzberger

*Will they be appreciated and cherished*
*By the next generation?*
*Will they be used by scholars*
*For the study and interpretation*
*Of music and poetry?*
*Will they be placed maybe*
*On the desks and shelves*
*Of people whom I will never encounter?*
*Or, will they be tossed into oblivion*
*By the rough hands of time*
*And be locked forever in death's pavilion?*

*I hope that somebody*
*Will be kind to me*
*And save my music and poetry*
*For posterity—*

# Epitaph

Look for my verse
In the archives of time,
Turning the battered
Yellow pages of old rhyme.

Although you never saw my face
Nor ever heard my name,
We still belong to the same
Invisible Power
Who destines our first
And last hour.

Friend of my spirit, be kind,
Read my song—
I am but a shadow
Of the past,
Leaving behind
Only a track of words.
Please, follow my lines,
Don't let them die—

Once I was also alive,
Filled with passion and drive,
Living with beauty
By my side.

# Magda Herzberger

*I rejoiced and cried,*
*And tried to reveal*
*The hidden wonders of life*
*Till the end of my strife—*

*Someday, when the cold*
*Eternal night*
*Will extinguish your flame*
*And cover forever your sight,*
*Encounter one another we might—*

# Finale

The poet's heart
Will never die—
It is connected to earth,
To sea and to the sky,
Recording the vibrations
Of the universe,
Through the free flow of verse—
The beat of rhyme
Can't be stopped by time,
To eternity it belongs.
It is life's pulse
And the rhythm of its songs.

Magda Herzberger

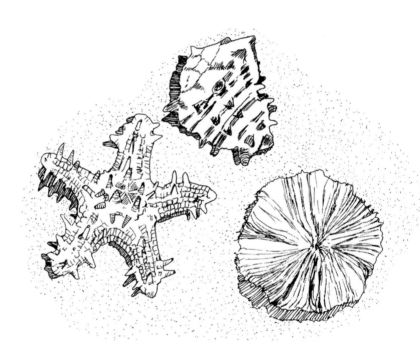

# Afterword

## A Look into the Life of the Sea

My dear readers, probably you will wonder why I included at the end of my book the following poems and the musical score of one of them: "Deity, Lord of the Sea." Both of these poems give an insight into the life, mystery, and the music of the sea.

Being a poet and a composer, I also wanted to share with you one of my more complex musical compositions. It demonstrates how music and poetry are strongly related.

Poetry is the music of the spoken words and music represents the symphony of life.

## At the Seashore

*There is a distant paradise*
*Exempt from winter's snow and ice,*
*Where velvety sand*
*Separates the water from the land,*
*Where friendly tall palms*
*Wave their long green arms,*
*Where white seagulls*
*Circle the blue sky,*
*Where the pelicans fly high,*
*Then they swoop down*
*With great rapidity*

## Magda Herzberger

To the surface of the sea,
And with their long flat beaks
Pull out from there the fish expertly.

My long-held wish finally came true
And I am sitting by the seashore,
Witnessing these wonders
And many more.

I am walking on the soft sand
Watching the waves undulating,
Bending, breaking, falling, rising,
And then hitting the shore
With a wild roar.
I feel happier than ever before!

But gradually
The sky becomes cloudy.
The water of the sea
Is losing its clear blue hue,
And a big zigzag sign
Is crossing the overcast sky,
Through and through.
The loud sound of thunder is heard,
The menace to every bird.
A blinding streak of light
Illuminates the bleak sky.

## Midnight Musings

The desperate cry of a sandpiper
In awe and despair,
Echoes in the air.

I look at the turbulent sea
Fighting with the stormy weather.
The big waves move faster and faster,
Getting higher and higher,
Jumping over each other,
Then crashing more and more
On the defenseless shore.

Torrents of big raindrops
Start falling steadily,
And the sea succumbs
To the storm's fury,
Letting it pass by finally.

A large blue patch appears
On the darkened sky,
Marking the end of turbulence
And the beginning of silence
Over water and land.

At the seashore I still stand,
Looking at the sunshine once more
Before I leave the battered shore.
But I will come back again
To this wondrous, constantly changing terrain.

Magda Herzberger

# Deity: Lord of the Sea

Listen to the ocean's roar,
Its wild waves invade the shore—
The white crests are rising high
And dark clouds obscure the sky—

On the sandy beach I stand
Where the water hits the land—
I hear seagulls' desperate cry
As Neptune is passing by—
Through the turbulence and noise
I detect a deafening voice:

"Listen to me
Whoever you may be,
I am the ancient God of the Sea!
Neptune is my name,
Did you ever hear
Of my deadly game?
My bad temper and anger
Evoke terror and fear.
There is death and destruction
Wherever I appear!
Humanity is begging
For my mercy and pity.
I left my sacred place

To meet you face to face,
And to remind you
That the legends never die—
My spirit is still around,
To my Blue Kingdom
I am forever bound—"

"Neptune, I know you well. Please
retreat into your ancient shell!
Control your fury!
You had your glory!
And let peace descend
Upon water and land—
Have compassion
In your heart.
Don't tear ships
And men apart!"

"Mortal, listen to me!
I can never rest,
I must cross relentlessly,
The vast sea's open breast,
And cast upon its body,
The raging tempest—

"I am controlled and directed
By a higher power—
I can't restrain my bad temper
Nor master my anger—

## Magda Herzberger

*I am destined to bring disaster,*
*Destruction and devastation,*
*To all the places of my destination—*
*I am the cursed spirit of the sea*
*And a part of eternity—*

*"Mortal, seek shelter,*
*And flee from me!*
*Flee from me!*
*I am a great menace*
*To humanity!*

*"Mortal, remember me!*
*Remember me!*
*Look through the pages*
*Of Roman mythology*
*And you will find me listed*
*As Neptune, the fierce God of the Sea."*

*As Neptune is leaving finally*
*The surface of the sea,*
*Blue patches appear gradually*
*In the storm-ridden sky—*
*The seagulls don't cry anymore*
*And peace descends*
*Upon the weather-beaten shore—*

NOTE: On the following pages is the full orchestral music for the poem "Deity: Lord of the Sea."

# Deity: Lord of the Sea
## Music & Lyrics by
# MAGDA HERZBERGER
## Arranged by FRANK METIS

For Mezzo Soprano and Bass Baritone
With S.A.T.B. Chorus and Piano Accompaniment

Duration: approx. 8:40

**Performance Notes:** According to Gustav Mahler, "What is best in music is not to be found in the notes!" His remark seems appropriate here because this arrangement is meant to express the essence of Magda Herzberger's eloquent tone poem, as conveyed by the conflicting emotions of the two leading characters and chorus. The stated metronome tempi are merely suggestive; it is the flow and feeling within each section that more likely will determine each tempo. Also, care should be taken that the transition from one segment into the next is smooth and seamless, with gradual tempo changes well performed in unison. The "sh___" effect by the chorus during the opening bars is meant to be reminiscent of ocean waves and blowing winds. Let it be *understated* and not overshadow the music. The *spoken* choral section at letter <u>M</u> should be delivered crisp and precise, carefully observing the dynamics and the *poco rit.* at the end. For optimum results, a well conducted rehearsal is recommended prior to public performance.

Frank Metis

# DEITY: LORD OF THE SEA

Music and Lyrics by:
MAGDA HERZBERGER

Arranged by:
FRANK METIS

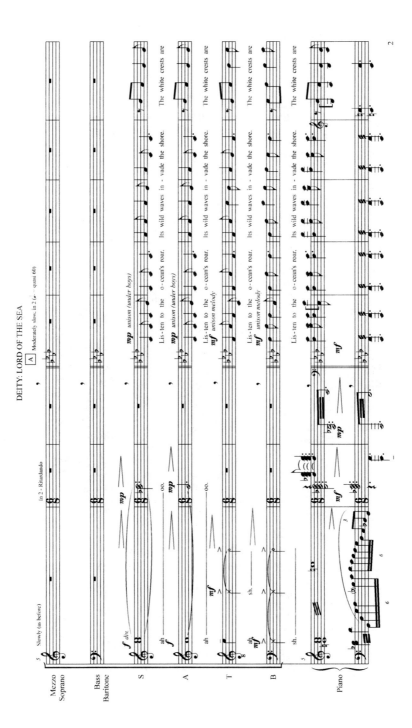

DEITY: LORD OF THE SEA

DEITY: LORD OF THE SEA

DEITY: LORD OF THE SEA

DEITY: LORD OF THE SEA

DEITY: LORD OF THE SEA

DEITY: LORD OF THE SEA

8

# DEITY: LORD OF THE SEA

DEITY: LORD OF THE SEA

10

DEITY: LORD OF THE SEA

DEITY: LORD OF THE SEA

12

DEITY: LORD OF THE SEA

Mezzo Soprano
Bass Baritone
S
A
T
B
Piano

*109*

vast sea's o - pen breast, And cast up - on its bod - y the rag - ing temp - est!

vast sea's o - pen breast, And cast up - on its bod - y the rag - ing temp - est!

I am con - trolled and di -

*p unis.* He is

*p unis.* He is

*p unis.* He is

*mf*

*somewhat rhythmic*

*ff*

13

DEITY: LORD OF THE SEA

14

DEITY: LORD OF THE SEA

15

DEITY: LORD OF THE SEA

DEITY: LORD OF THE SEA

172
O
Moderately, a tempo (♩ = quasi 80)
poco rit.
mf
mp
Mezzo Soprano
des - p'rate cry As Nep - tune is pass - ing by.
I will re - mem - ber! Yes!
Bass Baritone
Mor - tal, re - mem - ber me! Re - mem - ber me!
Look through the pag - es of
S
A
T
B
As Nep - tune is pass - ing by.
Piano

# DEITY: LORD OF THE SEA

DEITY: LORD OF THE SEA

21

## DEITY: LORD OF THE SEA

# About the Author

Magda Herzberger was born and raised in the city of Cluj, Romania. She is a poet, lecturer, composer, and the author of 11 previously published books: *The Waltz of the Shadows* (1st and 2nd Editions); *Eyewitness to Holocaust*; *Will You Still Love Me?*; *Songs of Life*; and her most recent works, *Survival*, the compelling autobiography of Magda's early life in Romania and her suffering at the hands of the Nazis; *Devotional Poetry*, dedicated to the readers of *Survival*; *Tales of the Magic Forest*; *If You Truly Love Me*, dedicated to her husband on their 60th wedding anniversary, *Dreamworld*, and *Transcript of 1980 Magda Herzberger Interview by the Wisconsin Historical Society*.

Magda was a marathon runner, skier, and mountain climber. She and her husband, Dr. Eugene E. Herzberger, a retired neurosurgeon, reside in Fountain Hills, Arizona.

_Magda Herzberger_

They have a daughter Monica, a son Henry, two grand-children, Mira Ma and Nathan, and one great-grand-daughter, Erzi Nicole.

Magda's primary goals are to instill love for poetry in the hearts of people through her work, to keep the memory of the Holocaust alive, and to show the beauty of life through her writings and music. Her philosophy of life: Have faith, hope, and love in your heart—believe in impossible dreams and make them come true—cherish each moment of life—and never take anything for granted.

Groundbreaking Press, publisher of _Midnight Musings_, _Dreamworld_, _If You Truly Love Me_, _Survival_, and _Transcript of 1980 Magda Herzberger Interview by the Wisconsin Historical Society_, also publishes the Second Edition of _The Waltz of the Shadows_, _Devotional Poetry_, and her first children's book, _Tales of the Magic Forest_.

Magda may be contacted at:
magdaherzberger@yahoo.com
www.magdaherzberger.com

# About the Illustrator

The cover and interior illustrations for *Midnight Musings* have been created by Monica A. Wolfson. Monica is Magda Herzberger's daughter. She also created the cover and inside illustrations for Magda's books: *Devotional Poetry, Tales of the Magic Forest, If You Truly Love Me,* and *Dreamworld.*

Monica has a Masters from Arizona State University in Educational Technology. She is also an accomplished singer, having performed in various venues, and having written and published her own songs and poetry. In addition to all of the above, she is a professional photographer.

Monica is married to Dave Wolfson, a transportation planner and committed storm chaser and photographer. They live in Fountain Hills, Arizona.

Monica can be contacted at:
monica@wolfsonworks.com
www.wolfsonworks.com

CPSIA information can be obtained at www.ICGtesting.com
Printed in the USA
BVOW07s1959180713

326357BV00001B/2/P